Uncommon KITCHENS

KITCHENS

Uncommon

A REVOLUTIONARY
APPROACH TO
THE MOST POPULAR
ROOM IN THE HOUSE

Sophie DONELSON

Abrams, New York

3 Leave Space for Change (It's the Only Constant) 126

4 Forget the Gut Reno … Do This Instead 180

COUNTERMOVEMENT

The most loved room in the house is in need of more love. Better love. Quite frankly: *Your* love.

We've officially reached *peak kitchen design*. We know exactly how to make a beautiful, luxurious cooking space. There are laypeople who can tell Calacatta from Carrara, who have a preferred rack configuration of their dishwashers, and who have strong opinions on the best shape of pendant to illuminate an island. Team: We've really developed a muscle for this!

And many among us are ready for a little more. A little more personality, a little more soul, a little more love for the loveliest room—the one with a bowl of apples, ice cream, and a light that stays on all night. It's the room of first-thing-in-the-morning conversations and late-night snacks, a room hardy enough to withstand dirty projects and tender enough to conjure childhood memories. The kitchen is no ordinary room.

For all the love and emotion we festoon on the kitchen, it doesn't always look it. Living rooms take on art and objects, soft furnishings to make them comfortable and welcoming; bedrooms often have family photos, a reminder of what happens at home, making family. But kitchens are often excused as workstations, prized for efficiency and cleanliness. We adorn the living room sofa with velvet cushions—tasseled if we're feeling kicky. But in the kitchen, it's: *This greige tile feels like a safe bet.*

An LA kitchen by Reath Design, with new colored-glass window panes and cheery Benjamin Moore French Horn 195 paint.

No wonder many of us find ourselves reminiscing about a family kitchen from growing up; not a perfect one, not a new or luxurious one, but one in which conversations happened, food was made, life unfolded. Homey, welcoming, ours. Perhaps you've found yourself in the corner of the internet that is exclusively the domain of British kitchens where skirted cabinets, plaster walls, and analog-looking ranges converge for a meeting of the unstoppably charming and unpretentiously chic. Nostalgia is a powerful drug, and you don't need an old family house nor a case of Anglophilia to recognize that homeyness is lacking from the current breed of kitchens.

We ask a lot from this room. Designer Meta Coleman cites one client's spot-on request that her kitchen be both a workhorse and a show pony. Nowhere else in the house are the twin criteria of aesthetics and performance in so much demand.

> "The kitchen must be both a workhorse and a show pony."

There are best practices for doing both, and more and better shopping options for appliances and surfaces than ever before. This is true for renters, too—IKEA has done a bang-up job with kitchens for years, creating freestanding islands and DIY elements that can be removed. Creating a kitchen that ticks the boxes—efficient/productive and pretty—is often within reach.

This book is about what's possible beyond that.

The point of architecture, design, and decoration—*the built environment* as it's called—is to create experiences within them. "We shape our buildings; thereafter they shape us," wrote Winston Churchill. This is not about looking good, certainly not to make an alluring photo, but about guiding our everyday actions, enriching the very marrow of life. At the very least, good design reduces the friction in our lives; at best, it enhances them profoundly.

To wit: consider the tiny, excruciating pain of touching the handle of a wobbly kitchen faucet or closing a cabinet door that won't shut properly. (A thousand tiny paper cuts a week, it feels like!) Now, how about that moment a soft-close drawer does its thing. Or even afternoon light falling across the countertops just so. There are grace notes all around.

The walk-in pantry of my own Montréal kitchen was a white box. Paint (Farrow & Ball India Yellow), and some cute trim (salvaged. . .1950s house) made it a sweet destination for storage and making coffee.

THERE ARE FOUR SPECIFIC WAYS to let design drive a better kitchen experience. (A better life experience!) And this goes for renters and renovators and everyone in between; employing color and pattern, treating the kitchen as a room first, designing with flexibility in mind, and working around the existing imperfect elements. This book holds illustrated examples of each, but these projects hardly stay in their lane. The kitchen is too hulking of a concept to be contained—its cross-category and its best design insights inform other rooms, too.

1 SECTION ONE is an argument for getting down with color. Why? Because color and pattern is a mood booster. Raise your hand if you've ever thought:

* A so-called CROWD-PLEASING choice isn't always a YOU-PLEASING choice.

* Why is pale gray considered a SAFE color? Are others DANGEROUS? Does hanging out with slate blue mean I've fallen into the WRONG CROWD?

* Designing for the potential future buyer of a home we might not even sell seems like . . . A TERRIBLE IDEA.

If you've thrown that fist in the air for three, two, one . . . or none, this part of the book is for you! Color acumen is something the kitchens in this section share, but that's not all they offer.

opposite

In Montréal, a breakfast room with a painting by Dan Schmidt, Circa Lighting pendant, pink lime-plaster walls, and a pop of color in the window: Benjamin Moore Split Pea.

SECTION TWO explores the idea of abandoning the rigidity of the modern but uniform dream kitchen, that turnkey entity with panel-covered appliances, tiers of cupboards running up the wall, and every element interconnected like an architectural bodysuit. (But was it ever a good idea for a blouse and underwear to be connected, you have to ask yourself.) The kitchen was once a room like any other, with movable furniture and lamps and decoration. We can learn from this.

IN SECTION THREE, we look at reintroducing flexibility so this room can grow and change alongside our needs and whims. This runs counter to the idea that kitchen decisions like surfaces, appliances, and storage are irreversible. Not so! There are innumerable ways to keep tinkering if you so decide.

SECTION FOUR will delight and excite renters and budget renovators especially with some extra-potent design wisdom—it's about working with what you've got. Why here? Because necessity is the mother of invention. Spaces with many limitations or few resources must rely on imagination and sheer will. The results can be beautiful.

What's happening today in kitchens is bigger than a countermovement. Us true believers want to marry the extraordinary things felt *inside* this beloved room with exuberant, hopeful aesthetics we can see. Kitchen happiness is generative—giving a bit of energy and love to this room all but guarantees future joyful experiences. The kitchen deserves this, but more importantly, so do you.

opposite

In a cabin by Commune Design in the San Gabriel Mountains outside Los Angeles are oak cabinets made with fine finger joinery.

Wow, They Really Went for It

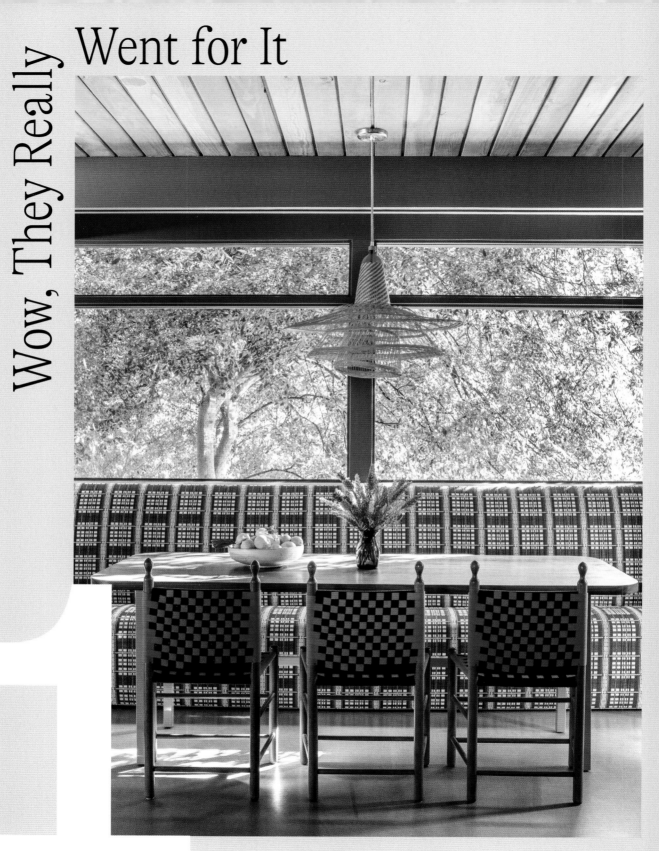

1

W e're not there yet, but it's on the way: the golden era of kitchen design. Finally, there's a crop of well-priced, pretty-cute appliances, tile, and surfaces that go beyond glossy gray and ivory, and a mounting understanding that we all use this space uniquely—one person's take-out destination is another person's challah bakery.

For decades, you couldn't spot a kitchen or bathroom in a design magazine—no one cared about the working rooms of the house it was said, only the decorated ones. The sixties had a brush with borderline kinky kitchen design with plaid-pattern refrigerators and whatnot. But the undercurrent was dark: If we make the kitchen cute, maybe women will want to stay there! The 1990s brought some relief; kitchen peoples (typically moms) were partially relieved of their arduous duties thanks to, oh, electric appliances and packaged foods (Lunchables, anyone?) and the room had, well, room to grow.

"Seeking the peace that comes with feeling nourished by your surroundings."

Foodies and amateur chefs gravitated toward industrial kitchen styling; stainless steel arrived and still dominates as an appliance finish. From TV cooking shows we adopted the kitchen stadium—appliances centered on the floor versus against the wall, and all eyes on the cook searing a Friday-night steak while chatting with guests at the island.

But lots more than food prep happens in the kitchen—it's the de facto space in most households for homework, and it's the natural place to host a friend or neighbor for coffee, be it at the kitchen table or perched at the island. The homey comforts

A kicky California project by Reath Design (more beginning page 16) has a banquette in a fabric by Knoll.

of farmhouse style made sense for all that. (That kitchen stadium concept, less so.) The vintage-inspired styling was pointedly unpretentious. Shaker-style cabinets and a primitive wood table were a nod at our agrarian roots and a reminder of the simple pleasures of life: harvest and commune. Ahem, even if the "harvest" was Domino's delivery.

Despite the newfound freedom to take from the room what you desire, a consensus emerged around a few core themes. Those Shaker cabinets, easy to manufacture and deemed "classic," stayed, so did appliances clad in stainless steel (or at least the look). And neutrals—'nuff said.

Was this because these details were so beguiling they made your heart sing? Hardly! On the contrary, they're simply "safe," which was key in the early 2000s when houses started being designed to flip.

But what fun is a kitchen designed for others? Who wants to wear someone else's clothing? So, even as the kitchen renovation conversation centered around return on investment, a countermovement said: No thanks! So long as this is my room for hosting friends and making toast, the only "return" worth seeking is simply satisfaction—little moments of joy and peace that come with feeling nourished by your surroundings. It's not just the toast that's fulfilling, it's the *smell* of toast, the table with crumbs, the birds outside the window, the people eating the toast . . . call it the toast experience.

"Close the screen, close your eyes, and conjure a kitchen that makes you feel happy. Start there with your mood board."

For those of us who get it, the quest for joy at home, especially in a room that gets messy and smelly, is the payoff itself, remunerated with feelings of hominess (hygge, we say now), many good meals, and the attendant memories. Not everyone's on board with this yet, but they're coming, give 'em time.

Ready to make a loving kitchen? Don't be deterred by the commitment or price tag—custom cabinetry and new counters are far from a necessity when it comes to perking up the room. But bits of color and pattern are an effective shortcut to good vibes. To misquote Kate Moss, nothing tastes as good as color feels.

So if you're renovating or rethinking your space and you have neutrals on your mind, ask yourself: Do you love the way you feel in a white or gray room, or has that look seeped into your consciousness like a trend lands in our closet despite not being germane to our style nor a

The upper New York State kitchen of an artist-musician couple includes an inky Mediterranean blue tiles and paint to match; it helps the bright ceramics and retro hardware pop.

particularly great idea? (Think: Prairie dresses.) Close the screen, close your eyes, and conjure a kitchen—or any room—that makes you feel warm and happy. Start there with your mood board.

When renters and homeowners tack in the direction of creativity and imagination, take note! It can be purely decorative, the type of project that can be undone by an afternoon of spackling or painting, like a gallery wall of friends' and family art (page 57) or as committed as shimmering pink tile (page 33) or I-dare-you colorful cabinetry (page 19). With intensely joyful color and whimsical touches, you won't need a sign that reminds you to live, love and laugh. It'll almost assuredly happen. There's no such thing as drudgery in a purple kitchen.

Calculated Color Risks Gone Right

Advice on

Designing
for messes

Choosing
daring colors

Making happy
compromises

This one is a defiant one: a kitchen that snubs the cues of its architecture and instead sinks into serotonin-laced sensations of color and pattern. If you've ever felt limited by the bones of your house—this one's for you.

There's always a dance between listening to the existing architecture (if it has integrity, of course) and renovating for modern life; this woodsy SoCal hideaway by Reath Design gets it just right. What works here is not taking the lines of home too seriously—a midcentury house can lean toward modesty, austerity even. There's a directive to play it cool, to traffic in neutrals, to leave the walls and floors unembellished. Instead, the folks behind this house said *meh* to the so-called best practices and followed their heart, tousling with the architectural elements until they felt downright playful—the trusses and beams are now wine-colored, and one is even used to catch copper pots on S-hooks.

Architecture of this period can be cool and standoffish, and in a kitchen, the impact is often deepened, but oriental rugs make quick work of homeyness, same for fresh hues like the emerald cabinetry and powder-blue range. Making a lively female-led design from lines that would indicate otherwise would seem the victory here, but there's more than meets the eye: The decor choices cleverly allow for cooking messes, collections and passions, and everyday life to unfold without detracting from the space. In other words: You don't have to keep this kitchen perfect in order to enjoy it.

above

Concessions must be made! There's no range hood here because it would have obstructed the view. Instead, the owner opens the window when she cooks.

opposite

The countertop marble continues up the walls; it can stain, but it ages beautifully, like an old bistro table would.

"DECOR CHOICES that cleverly allow for everyday life to unfold— without detracting from the space."

above

The adjacent dining room
is decked in a wallpaper
from Jennifer Shorto, a
cult wallpaper brand. In
this pattern, Oranges &
Leaves, phantasmagoric
cities emerge from
peeled-open oranges.

opposite

A Soane textile is draped
on a console table in
the dining room, looking
toward the kitchen.

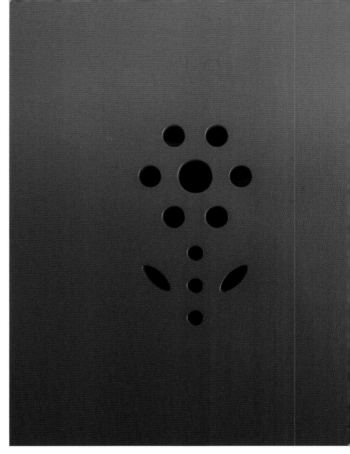

Frances Merrill
of Reath Design

Design the kitchen for doing more than just CHOPPING.

There's enough drudgery in the kitchen, there can be enjoyment, too, so put something in there that signals leisure, like art or furniture.

Old-house kitchens aren't meant to be OPEN.

If you modernize an old home, ask yourself: If the kitchen was intended to be a *public space* when this house was built (most weren't), what would that look like? It might echo the same lines as elsewhere in the house, such as an arch or another architectural detail.

Consider what you *WANT*, not what you've *seen*.

For some, the dream is the English country kitchen with comfy chairs and a work table. Others actually *want* to be alone in the kitchen. Don't just look at other references; think about how you want to live.

There are NO QUICK TIPS for choosing color and pattern.

It's a combination of preparation and taking a risk. Spend time thinking about it, but also be prepared to jump in.

Get to KNOW all your stuff.

The designers behind this kitchen inventory and photograph *every single item* meant to go into a cabinet or drawer. Measure the tallest bottle before choosing shelf height. Consider where your heaviest Dutch oven will go—ideally somewhere you don't need to bend to retrieve it.

ARE YOU messy or neat?

A combination of open and closed storage works best for most people. If you like to see what you have—and you're tidy—then more open shelves can work. Are you messy? Color and pattern can help. The more you have going on, the more color and pattern can distract your eye from the mess.

A big sink can help you RELAX.

You don't always want a kitchen that must be completely tidied every night. Put the dishes into one big, deep sink so you don't have to look at them; your design choices can help you sit down at the end of the day.

Make CONCESSIONS.

Don't ever squeeze something in just to check a box—like a banquette if it just doesn't fit. You have to make choices, and that's OK.

You don't need ALL THE THINGS they say you're supposed to have.

Not every kitchen needs a hood—this kitchen has a window that opens instead.

KNOW your "thing."

A warming drawer, a trash compactor, maybe you're wed to something, so go ahead and keep it. Just know it about yourself: What is *your thing*?

When renovating, STRIVE for creative solutions.

Painting your subfloor is going to last a lot longer than installing a so-called "sustainable" flooring like bamboo. It's sold as eco-friendly, but nothing that has a short shelf life is eco-responsible.

Section One

CHAPTER 2

An Internet-Famous Rental

"If you want the truth, the cabinets are IKEA," began Nicolò Castellini Baldissera, the debonair Italian designer and entrepreneur, as if letting go of a well-guarded secret. An aristocratic aesthete's Milan kitchen, outfitted with a Grand Tour's worth of treasures . . . and big-box-store cabinets? Shocking, but not surprising, as they say. But who's looking at the cabinets when the room is laden with found beauty: ancient tiles and etchings and Murano glass. And yes, a stove. "For myself and other home cooks like my clients, I prefer a space that appears to have been there a long time. As a designer, I love to create an environment with a past—even if that past maybe never existed!" he explains.

The irony of this very lived-in and loved room is that Nicolò is only camped out here for a time. But renting didn't keep him from digging in his heels decoratively—after all, the treasures and appliances will journey on with him to the next destination. In Europe, it's common for your appliances to go with you when you move, even among rentals. That pieced-together look that many of us find so *charmant* is merely a byproduct of the comings and goings of things and the need to make it work without commissioning new fitted cabinets for the space.

The particular magpie-classicist patchwork of Nicolò's kitchen packs extraordinarily well. The objects come from far and wide, and he takes enormous joy in reconfiguring them to be functional (a pyramidal chest of drawers holds the flatware). So no wonder that when Nicolò hosts, it's here. "The kitchen table is just large enough to seat six for a cozy supper, which is what happens most of the time—we never use the dining room."

The Milan kitchen of designer, entrepreneur, and C&C Milano textiles executive Nicolò Castellini Baldissera. An enormous dining room closet holds china and hand-blown glassware. The Toucan prints hung in the Milan bathroom of Nicolò's great grandmother, Lia Portaluppi, wife of architect Piero Portaluppi who created the iconic Villa Necchi Campiglio, made even more famous from films like *House of Gucci* and *I Am Love*.

"A NAME-BRAND CUSTOM kitchen just announces that you've spent $200,000. Buy a painting instead! A super-sleek built-in kitchen can be wonderful for chefs, but they're lacking in atmosphere."

Section One

"I LOVE LARGE FRIDGES, I can't stand the standard size; it's quite American of me. My family always had a big Kelvinator, and when I first moved to London in the late '80s, my house came with a large double fridge, and now it's something that I will never give up. That's my luxury."

Uncommon Kitchens

left

In lieu of cupboards is a freestanding hutch fashioned from antique gates; it holds everyday china, tools, and small appliances. The dining chairs are from Nicolò's Casa Tosca home line, which is produced in his hometown Milan and his second home, Tangier, where he enlisted a rattan artisan to create pieces similar to ones in the home in which he was raised.

opposite

The ten-drawer pyramidal chest holds flatware and other kitchen tools. A Victorian-looking ball sits on top. The antique tiles are from Salerno.

Nicolò Castellini Baldissera

designer *and* entrepreneur

MILAN

RECYCLE and RELOCATE things.

I like the idea of a kitchen put together with bits and pieces from life. I have several storage units with remains of a more glorious past. Everything in my house is traveled. Sometimes a rather long way!

Buy better-than-average quality appliances and KEEP THEM.

When we move from this rental, we'll take with us as much as possible—my cooker, big fridge, most of the appliances, as I bought them with the intention of bringing them with me.

For storage, think BEYOND CABINETS.

Cabinets can break a space in half, and when there are lots of them, you feel inclined to fill them up. Having less space forces you to organize yourself better. Try storing your cups and dishes in a cupboard in an adjacent room, or use a small set of drawers for flatware. It doesn't have to be kitchen furniture per se.

Hang a plate or tiles or LESS-PRECIOUS pictures

that can suffer the fumes or the steam. You should have art in the kitchen; it's fun to sit around and see something that you normally don't see in the kitchen.

"**A RUG IN THE KITCHEN,** that's one thing I can't stand! It's my only hygienic thing . . . a floor in the kitchen must be clean in the best possible way, so the idea of germs and debris, I find it rather disgusting. Funnily, I break my own rule for the dining room, where you sometimes need it to combat noise. But I try to do that with curtains, not rugs."

Section One

31

Making Room for Pretty

Advice on

New materials
in an old house

Reorienting
the workflow

Streamlining
the number
of surface
materials

What's the difference between a house deemed a tear-down and another with character? Imagination, really! Sometimes all it takes to resurrect an offbeat house into something sublime is creativity. That's what happened in this 1966 one-off so called "mini-estate" in LA's lush-but-central Fryman Canyon: The movie exec owners and their designer, Jaqui Seerman, didn't fall prey to makeover madness despite the opinion of friends and professionals. Instead, they kept the good-if-challenging parts of the house, such as the plank-cedar ceilings and walls and layered in other design elements they craved, such as sexy peach-colored tile and brass fittings. Who says you have to choose?

left

Atop the polished marble backsplash is a shelf and brass rail supported by antique brass shelf brackets in a beehive motif.

opposite

The room is divided into a cooking area and a cleanup area; this is the primary sink with a Waterworks faucet; there's a prep sink near the range to down on trips across the kitchen.

following pages

The designer turned to the super-cool shops in the West Hollywood design district for the project: The vintage four-globe pendant light is from Harbinger, and dining chairs are by Peter Dunham of Hollywood at Home; the textiles (Fig Leaf) are also his. The floor tiles are Lorca marble from Tabarka Studio.

left

The designer was briefly stumped about how to address the hood—there were already a lot of materials in the kitchen. To minimize visual clutter, she opted to use the same field tiles and a brass cap.

opposite

The peach-colored glossy crackle field tile is from Waterworks.

Jaqui Seerman
designer

It's OK to ignore the chorus.

The old cedar ceilings provoked a plethora of suggestions: Bleach it! Paint it! Demo it! But for a design to be a beautiful backdrop for life, it has to connect with its environment, and that cedar is part of the integrity of the house, and the house connects to the landscape here.

Make the central hub useful and PERSONAL.

It doesn't always need to be an island. A dining table does what an island can do and more. This table gets stacked with apps and snacks at a party, but frequently hosts meetings for the family staff: executive assistants, nanny, dog walker, and so on.

RETHINK the "work triangle."

Older houses sometimes force this decision: Not every space can accommodate a work triangle. It's OK to rethink the layout. Here there's a food-prep side (range, fridge, bar sink) and a cleanup side (dishwasher, kitchen sink). It's not conventional, but it's functional.

Repetition WORKS.

If you have a good thing going with your materials palette, stick with it. A statement hood (like in copper, for example) would add even more materials to this room, but tapping on tile and brass, which already existed throughout, added to the continuity of the space.

Let inspiration manifest in STRANGE ways.

The jumping-off point for this room scheme was an old Ralph Lauren campaign image, a picnic scene in a lush meadow, hence the cabinetry color. The brass hardware is a sort-of stand-in for equestrian gear.

"THEY KEPT THE good-if-challenging parts and layered in other design elements they craved—sexy peach-colored tile and brass fittings."

No Baking Required

What if we liberated the kitchen from cooking? Forgot the refrigerator-sink-stove "work triangle" and just enjoyed the space as the best room in the house for snacks? It's a concept that Colombe Studio, a Warsaw design firm, is exploring.

"More and more people admit to never cooking," says founder Marta Chrapka. "When we don't have that obligation—when cooking becomes a hobby—the kitchen can become even more attractive and interesting," she says. "We're always asking ourselves what sort of cabinets do you even need if you're dining from delivery."

What's cool about Colombe rooms is that they elicit conviviality and food-fueled camaraderie—and most have functions for home chefs—but few are held hostage by the tasks of food prep. The next few pages of Colombe projects shows a range of kitchens that feel free from chores—though each of the kitchens would make a lovely backdrop for them.

left

Onions and potatoes were typically kept in baskets to let them breathe. Bring this back!

opposite

The demand for painted wood cabinetry in old-world shapes is high; the Colombe team created a firm called Coucou Cabinets to make these profiles and ship them worldwide.

opposite

Floating brackets (instead
of typical slab shelves)
add utility to the space
and feel intentional and
architectural but unique.

above

Open storage allows for
flexibility—arrange art,
memento, spices . . . and
change it based on the
season or your mood.

left

In Marta's own apartment is a melange of client leftovers and unwanted items that she deemed worth keeping, such as this coral chandelier. The space was pulled together quickly and loosely.

below

Buy attractive things for organization and clean-up and then enjoy them by installing a little brass rail with S-hooks. It's decoration, but handy.

opposite

Two mismatched pendant lights hang over a wood counter that was moved here from a previous home. Without enough material, she used black granite on the adjacent surface and again on the backsplash. The mint surface is a wallpaper.

previous pages

A kitchen designed as a backdrop for piano concerts—that was the brief for this Warsaw kitchen. The art is an oversize hand-painted wallpaper panel from de Gournay. The cement floor tiles are new but were common in the year of build, 1913.

this page

Built with longevity in mind, this kitchen is on its second renovation. The black steel cabinetry stayed and the green cabinets evolved to a new hue. A hood is tucked in the steel frame.

Marta Chrapka
of Colombe Studio

WARSAW, POLAND

Start with an idea about DESIGN, not function.

Begin with inspiration—it could be Josef Frank furniture for example. And then consider the story of the people who live there. What's your way of living, how do you want to feel in the space?

For a kitchen to be COZY, it needs the right light,

plus fabrics to make the interior softer, and colors, which are especially powerful when dark. Those elements combine to create a feeling of being safe.

BANISH long countertops.

They keep you from moving naturally; everything feels too far away. One meter in length feels just right.

One color trick that's quite easy is to choose paints with NATURAL pigments,

because these were the coloring agents that were available at the time of older home builds. This makes a color believable in a vintage home.

To REINVENT your kitchen again and again, use wood cabinets.

You can repaint them and move the boxes into different configurations. Modern kitchen cabinet materials like MDF and polyurethane paints look plastic, wear out quickly, and can't be restored. The inability to age things well somehow deprives us of our heritage!

Bright light doesn't need to be overhead or be BRIGHT white.

Direct lighting is good for where you chop, but spotlights aren't the only solution. Lighting is very personal, but even LEDs offer different temperatures, so go warmer than the strong white or blue-tinted ones that are so common. Also: dimmers everywhere.

Food needs to BREATHE.

The cut-out shapes in cabinet doors is a nineteenth-century detail, and it's specifically for food ventilation. Even when you're using wood cabinets and natural paints, there's a specific smell inside. It's better for food when it's ventilated—hence the holes.

Decoration can also be USEFUL.

Hang peg railings with necessary but beautiful equipment such as a feather duster or linen cloths.

We have to LET GO of the fears

about what our parents will say. I once created a project for a man who bought fresh food—cheese, bread, wine—and ate it straight away—there was no fridge, no stove. These creative kitchens will happen, we're moving closer, but we can't be beholden to other people's opinions.

Section One

49

The Unrelenting Sweetness of the Breakfast Room Banquette

ADMITTEDLY, I'M DEAD WRONG ABOUT THIS ONE.

When I was editor of *House Beautiful* magazine, we dined out on breakfast rooms. Sun streaming into mullioned windows, plump floral pillows on a banquette, the ticking tablecloths, the block-print napkins, and daffodils in pitchers . . . croissants and bowls of berries and and and! Breakfast rooms are the centerfolds of design magazines, provoking unabated lust and feverish fantasies in readers. The images are screenshotted and saved in folders named "Dream House" or "Maybe Some Day!" or just: "LOVE!" They are coveted.

If there is one defining feature of the breakfast room, it's the banquette, or built-in bench seating, which in the last decade seemed to become as essential to a Fully Realized American Kitchen as a sink.

"Breakfast rooms are the centerfolds of design magazines, provoking unabated lust and feverish fantasies in readers."

Back in New York, just before I became complicit in brewing the breakfast room Kool-Aid, I was drinking it. I asked my designer Lys for an L-shaped one under the grand window in our not-so-grand Queens apartment and she refused. It's limiting, she countered: You can't move most of them, they serve only one purpose, and frankly, it cuts down options for rearranging. I came around to a table and chairs and lived happily with them; in fact, I still have them. A bit defensive perhaps, I started to dismiss the banquette as one of those parasitic trends that finds its way into the collective bloodstream and lives and lives.

Our move to Montréal, to my first *house*, meant my first-ever breakfast nook, and when I started crowdsourcing opinions for its layout, I was barraged by Team Banquette—from old readers, from A-list designers, from passionate civilians. I playfully but staunchly fought it, but boy, was the chorus formidable.

And so I looked hard at the idea—not for myself (I landed on the same table and some new-to-me chairs), but for its cultural vice-grip on design lovers. What I found was . . . cute. I saw the promise of squishing in a litter of little kids at snack time. The echoes of a child-hood bedroom window seat built for two. Bench-style back seats in 1970s station wagons. Vinyl diner booths. Nostalgia.

How many pieces of furniture elicit a downright emotional response? Few. When else does upholstery harken the sweetness of a baby animal nuzzling its sibling? Never. And so the breakfast room banquette lives on to charm another day.

In the Puget Sound is a
breakfast nook by designer
Heidi Caillier. The paint
color is Farrow & Ball
Down Pipe.

CHAPTER 5

Radical Terrazzo Designed to Last

All the way from the West Coast of Australia comes this testament to going all out. Here's what's amazing about this spot: While others might commit to black-and-white terrazzo and say, "that's a lot of look, I'll stop there," this homeowner, spunky Aussie fashion designer Poppy Lissiman, kept layering on the love with oodles of art by family and friends (as well as her own) and creative flourishes that keep joyfulness dotted throughout the home.

Lots of the houses here in Fremantle, near Perth on Australia's West Coast, are lovingly clad with terrazzo and terra-cotta—the legacy of Italian and Greek immigrant builders whose home countries provided those cheap and plentiful materials during the midcentury. Poppy was shopping for one of the region's low-slung modernist homes, but when she landed in a 1990s Tuscan-style villa with gracious grounds, she didn't fight it. Instead, she kept the terra-cotta floors (and nearly everything with integrity in the house) and added what she missed: a head-turning terrazzo befitting of her exuberant style.

Advice on

Reconciling
trend and
longevity

Living in an
investment
property

Room to grow
and change

opposite

Fashion designer Poppy Lissiman's Fremantle, Australia, kitchen is a spate of bold materials and boisterous art, but the palette keeps it all in check. Original terra-cotta floors, laminate-front cabinets, and—zing!—a terrazzo known as Santa Margherita Palladio Moro is what's happening here.

above

An olive tree grows in Poppy's courtyard. Lovely Australia!

Section One

53

left

The bar sink doesn't get much action—it mostly gets filled with ice for parties. The painting was an estate auction find that Poppy had reframed. The vase is by Memor Studio.

opposite

The natural wood-framed ceiling and wood window trim were existing. The cookware is mostly tucked away, not displayed like the art and books, because Poppy's husband, a passionate chef, buys what he considers the best of everything versus sets of things that might look consistent together.

"**TERRAZZO AND TERRA-COTTA**—the legacy of the Italian and Greek builders in the midcentury—define the space."

opposite
and right

The book rail keeps art books in rotation—a dynamic, moving display. Poppy spotted the idea online. The art over the mantel is by indigenous artist John Prince Siddon, a favorite of Poppy and her husband.

above

An enormous leather banquette faces the terrace. The vintage chairs are the iconic Marcel Breuer Cesca style. The gallery wall showcases the newest and most loved in the homeowners' growing collection of art.

"FIRST, USE WHAT'S
on hand—it's responsible
and it just makes sense."

Poppy Lissiman
fashion designer

Throw your PERSONALITY into it,

even if you might resell some day. The pool of buyers will be slightly limited, but you'll enjoy living in it until then. (Plus, a motivated buyer will make their own changes regardless.)

For everything permanent: Stick to a consistent PALETTE.

The wall color, art, rugs can all be changed, but you can still go bold for the permanent parts (counters, floors) so long as you stick to a consistent palette, like black and white, which is easy to complement.

It's OK to break CONSISTENCY.

The window trim throughout the home is painted white, but it didn't look right in the kitchen. It's painted black now, which feels natural for being close to the terrazzo. You don't have to adhere to one idea just because it works in most places.

Big furniture makes a room look BIGGER.

A banquette that fills a room seems huge (this one seats eighteen), but it actually makes the space look bigger.

REUSE whatever materials you can.

If something is beautiful, if it has integrity, find a way to use it—it's responsible, and it just makes sense that you'd first use what's on hand.

Allow your taste to MATURE; leave room to grow.

If you shop resale furniture, you can swap things in and out, buying and reselling. Tastes grow and change, and you want a house that can change alongside you.

Don't forget MAGAZINES!

My search for a specific material went in circles until I stumbled on the stone's formal name and its vendor in a magazine. Buy magazines you wouldn't normally buy—you never know where you're going to find your answers.

Let your builder or contractor choose the SUBCONTRACTORS.

Don't bother researching and hiring your own subcontractors or getting recommendations from friends—the builder's will always be better, will show up, and will get along with the team.

Small city and limited materials options? GOOD.

Bigger cities offer more showrooms, but in a smaller city, there's only the stuff you don't want and then a few things you might like. It cuts down on choice and makes it quite easy!

Going BOLD feels different than it looks.

Terrazzo is quite punchy and loud, but when you're living in the space, it works. Terrazzo and tile options are a sea of gray, so it was special to find something so purely black and white.

A Fancy DIY in South London

File under

Small space,
big impact

Bougie DIY

Budget-friendly
brilliance

Look closely: Yellow painter's tape and two creative minds are the ingredients behind this cheerful London flat. The room is remarkably budget-friendly with IKEA base units, ceramic tile applied vertically, and vintage lighting—OK, and then there's a seating-area splurge, a pair of 1950s French rope-and-oak chairs, the type of piece found at the galleries of one of the owners, antiques dealer Dorian Caffot de Fawes. His husband, Thomas Daviet, an interior designer, came up with the paper-tape idea and stands by its durability—and reversibility.

The yellow stripes were inspired by the striped towels and striped umbrellas at Hotel Il Pellicano on the Tuscan seaside, a yearly, glamorous getaway for the owners: "It's smart and prestigious and somehow very casual and chic at the same time. Slim Aarons did a book about it! It's iconic!" says Dorian. The gentlemen's apartment is in a cool, old building where the units are connected by long, narrow balconies encircling an interior courtyard. When you arrive from the courtyard as they mostly do, you're greeted with a hit of cheerful yellow, a fitting antidote to the climate. "You're welcomed with a splash of sunshine," says Dorian.

Parts of the flat were already beautiful on their own—or almost were. Upon their visit, the floors were carpeted, but while Dorian distracted the agent, Thomas pulled up a discreet corner of carpet and saw herringbone parquet floors. Just how much of the original floor was there and how much of it was intact was a mystery until the renovation. Answer: It's the whole darn thing, kitchen and bathrooms included.

Those floors bring an elegance to the kitchen, a room people clamor to be in. "People pick up on the nonformal quality of a kitchen versus a dining room or even a sitting room," says Dorian. "Nonintimidating, welcoming, casual . . . in most homes I visit, and certainly here, it's the most relaxed room in the house."

The counters are a small square black tile that looks and wears better than the budget butcher block there previously. The herringbone parquet flooring was original to the place—it was stripped and stained. The photo is by French photographer Orlan; the chairs are vintage by the French designers Audoux-Minet.

Dorian Caffot de Fawes
antiquaire

Thomas Daviet
designer

LONDON

Stripe maintenance is EASY.

The paper tape (known as washi tape or painter's tape) almost never needs replacing. Areas with wear can be peeled away and replaced. Just keep a few spare rolls on hand.

Yellow—because LONDON!

We needed a bit of sun here. The moment you enter the house you're welcomed with a splash of sunshine.

To make ceramic tile look LESS builder-y,

install it vertically. It has a retro-swimming-pool vibe and feels totally different than the standard horizontal application.

Try vertical—not horizontal—STRIPES to slow down the eye.

Here, the yellow catches the attention, but the orientation of the stripes is actually calming. Horizontal stripes are called racer stripes for a reason!

MATCH the tile width and stripe width.

To the eye, it looks like a harmonious single line from top to bottom. When you mix materials, it's helpful to have that pleasing consistency.

A galley kitchen has ONLY one purpose.

But when you trade a chunk of wall space in favor of a sitting area, you increase the value of the room. Breakfast and lunch happen here, as well as bill-paying and household tasks. At night, Thomas can enjoy wine at the table while Dorian cooks.

You need tabletop LIGHTING.

Always do a table lamp in the kitchen. When that's missing in a kitchen, it can feel cold or unwelcoming. Lamps at eye-level bring warmth to the room that overheads and under-counter strips cannot.

Kitchens are universally WELCOMING

because they're the least formal rooms in the house. It's not intimidating to visit a kitchen—you can be equally comfortable in a client's kitchen or a neighbor's kitchen, it's that kind of room.

CHAPTER 7

A Fiery Snub to "Safe" Choices

What were you taught to hate? Yellow pine floors? Popcorn ceilings? Rugs with high pile? Here's a kitchen that looks at materials that others have left for dead and says: Hey! Easy on the judgments . . . let's have a fresh look.

Laminate cabinet fronts: check—beautiful hues and user-friendly. Back-painted glass: Back from the dead and looking as chic as any backsplash. Simple wood door and drawer pulls: hits from the '60s, '80s, and today; a comeback classic. Popcorn ceiling: You didn't even notice it, did you? In a room as vibrant as this, it'll never be the first thing you spot.

This is the kitchen of a 1964 rambler in Minnesota, owned by a couple who knows exactly what they love—brazen color and great appliances (and they love them enough to enjoy them front and center). They worked with a design team open to ideas that others had shunted aside long ago.

The space started as an open-plan—and too big to feel cozy. "Big is not always an asset; it can be hard to make a large, open kitchen feel welcoming," says Victoria Sass, whose Minneapolis-based Prospect Refuge Studio designed the space. "The best rooms are human-size—they're rooms you feel relaxed in." Architecture tells you how to feel, she explains. High ceilings can send a signal of being lofty and impressive, "which is great if your aim is to impress visitors or create a sense of awe," she says. But lower ceilings and smaller rooms are often associated with comfort, so that's what they went for. The addition of a powder room tightened up the floor plan, while using different materials or colors for the island and cabinets makes the room feel more organic, and less like a "set."

Revisiting those overlooked materials was a boon to the budget, too. Nothing is inherently bad, nothing inherently good, the designer explains, it's all what you make with it. Readers: All bets are off—enjoy your newfound freedom!

File under

A radical retrofit

Brave color

Throwback materials

opposite

The oak island is inspired by Alvar Aalto, a look accentuated by the blue drawer pulls; it's stained in Valspar Red Oak; the countertop is a Formica laminate. Over the sink is the iconic Louis Poulsen PH5 mini pendant in red.

following pages

The flat-panel cabinetry is the star here. It has contrasting colors: Benjamin Moore Dunmore Green on the bottom and Sherwin-Williams Flower Pot on top. The range, refrigerators, and dishwasher are all Fisher & Paykel. The couple likes the style of the fridge as is—they had no interest in a panelled version. The island stools are CB2. Over the island is a pendant by Rich Brilliant Willing.

Section One

this page

A slim rail running the length of the kitchen offers a lot of utility (spices, decorative bowls) and a place to display and swap out personal effects.

"**THINK TWICE** before removing something old. The one thing we can't make more of is time."

left

What's the obsession with hiding appliances? In the '50s and '60s, when small appliances were all the rage, they were proudly displayed. Why not buy ones you like and show them?

opposite

Who wouldn't be happy pouring a bevvie here? The bar surface is clad in copper; the funky wallpaper is by House of Hackney.

"**NOTHING IS** inherently bad, nothing inherently good, it's all what you make with it."

Make inexpensive materials look LUXURIOUS.

Show off their best feature by pairing them with a contrasting element. Round wood drawer pulls and glossy paint. You'll notice the loveliness of each element because of what it sits next to.

There's honesty in leaving your TOASTER out.

People are obsessed with hiding their small appliances, but it wasn't always like that. In the 1950s, people were proud of their gadgets—and I see that happening again; these homeowners love their Fisher & Paykel fridge and their toaster oven. It's very *come as you are* here.

There are two AUTHORS in every house, the architect and the resident.

A lot of conversation today is: How is this space going to work for ME? But we also need to support the house and its ideas—the space won't have a life unless you let it have its own, too. Relinquishing a little control allows a home to show its soul. And that's the beauty of it—you can't totally predict what you're going to get!

A "statement" over-island light is OVERRATED.

It puts a LOT of pressure on a single item. Aim for interesting moments baked into the rest of the room, not spending all the money and energy on one object.

You can measure and plan—or you can let SERENDIPITY take over.

Say you didn't account for your tallest olive oil bottle, you might find yourself in the supermarket researching new olive oils, maybe find something you love because your house sent you here.

The best colors take more than three words to DESCRIBE.

A muddy blueish, gray. Or, even better: when you start using words that aren't color-related, such as describing a sunset or a storm—when you're chasing a thought.

A good kitchen is a BESPOKE kitchen—

bespoke means made for you. It means that not everyone will like it. Lots of designed kitchens have the stone of the moment, the cabinet color of the moment, but anyone could live in that house and would like it fine. What's missing in that sort of home is *you*.

To make colors interesting, let them FIGHT.

Using two greens or two reds that don't quite match adds tension and complexity. When colors aren't exactly right together, they create an argument, and that's when design gets interesting!

HARDWARE: Don't discount the cheapos!

A lot of brilliant hardware, like simple wood handles, is totally dismissed, written off because it's two dollars a handle. Lots of it is thoughtfully designed and durable. Price is not always an indicator of quality—don't let that stigma get in the way of a great pick.

Section One

73

It's a Room First, a Kitchen Second

Bedroom, bathroom, living room . . . *kitchen*. It's no wonder we treat it differently than other rooms, even its name sets it apart. But the key to unlocking happiness in the kitchen—arguably our home's most enjoyable space (this is the domain of snacks, after all)—lies in addressing it like any other room.

You've probably had this experience: a visit to a home that's beguiling or cheerful, layered with colors or art or personal collections, and a sense of place. Maybe you toured the living rooms and then landed in the kitchen and ooof, it's a white box. What happened here? Did the paint run out, were there no vases left to festoon a windowsill, did the owners simply run out of energy? Or have we been taught that we can get by on functionality alone?

Admittedly, this room means business: appliances hum, counters need cleaning. There's always work to be done. And maybe for that reason, the kitchen often suffers from a lack of the imagination and playfulness we lavish on other rooms. But the sheer number of hours we spend here is the argument for decorative flights of fancy. If you're going to spend time there, make it a place that feels joyful and nourishing, not simply organized and clean.

The good news is that we instinctively know how to do this. Even if you only ambiently tune into design media, you've still likely absorbed the key truths of interior decorating. Count them off with me:

> "This room means business—but it also deserves the imagination and playfulness we lavish on other rooms."

opposite

A nod to freestanding furniture by Illinois firm Park & Oak.

Section Two

75

- ✳ **Fearlessly mix HIGH AND LOW**
- ✳ **Pair OLD AND NEW (thrift finds and heirlooms with IKEA and a splurge)**
- ✳ **Create a FLOOR PLAN that's intimate enough to invite conversation**
- ✳ **Invest in COMFORT over trend**
- ✳ **Incorporate COLOR—even a splash**
- ✳ **Vary SHAPES and TEXTURES**
- ✳ **Add something SENTIMENTAL OR PERSONAL to make it yours**

Sound familiar? These tenets haven't evolved much since Edith Wharton was writing about houses—they stick around because they work! This is how to create a happy a room that also happens to be a kitchen. And that's the ticket.

Let's address a few winning solutions.

SHAPE. This room lives for rectangles: fridge, oven, island, countertop. There's a disproportionate amount of boxy and clunky elements here; it's a real drag. So rope in something that's not linear. Add a few circular or shapely elements like globe-shaped pendant lighting, a round table, or a shelf of bowls, tea kettles, vases, or other unexpected shapes. "Break it up" is something decorators say a lot—you don't want to feel bound by straight lines, how square!

MATERIAL. All those smooth surfaces and hard edges deserve softness and texture. Curtains, blinds, or even upholstery, yes, is a solution. A bench with a seat cushion, a basket with a stack of dish towels, a skirted sink. A rug in the kitchen? Talk about a lightning rod topic . . . some people are icked out. But those who espouse it swear by a rug's noise-canceling properties, its ability to pull together a space, and the comfort it delivers—and they're OK with maintenance. (Indoor-outdoor rugs and washable systems like Ruggable are great solutions.) A crock of wooden spoons—shapely, organic—can lend some love, too.

SCALE. People gravitate to snug spaces; there's a feeling of safety and wellness in being somewhere human-sized. If you're renovating or planning a new space, think carefully about how big you go. Case in point: islands. Lately, they've so ballooned in size they're being dubbed *kitchen archipelagos*. You can't even pass a bowl of guacamole across them, and that's a travesty because everyone loves guacamole. Islands began as a casual gather-round spot, and they work well that way. They fail when they're so large they become a behemoth barrier to skirt around.

PERSONAL TOUCHES. There are tons of potential personal effects to be shared in this room. A decorative plate bought on a trip, hand-me-down china or an old teapot, or even a favorite plant or cut flowers. Kitchens that feel room-like tend to display the things we love. It doesn't take much.

OLD STUFF. This is easy to pull off. Old cabinets and old appliances (though workhorses they are!) probably aren't going to be a fit for you, but a decorative touch that speaks to age is a powerful element in a room. Try one of these: an old mirror to bounce around light, a farmhouse table, a rustic bowl, a secretary or small hutch for paperwork and correspondence . . . there's comfort in living with older things.

The point is this: The kitchen is a room like any other room, don't let its name stop you from tapping into your design and living intuition. Cheers, you've got this.

THIS ROOM LIVES FOR rectangles: fridge, oven, island, countertops—it's a real drag. So rope in a few circular or shapely elements—don't be bound by straight lines; how square!

following pages

The Connecticut kitchen of style renegade Eva Chen, designed by Hendricks Churchill with a Plain English work table and painted beadboard walls.

New World Anglophilia

The house was such a disaster: dank and dark, wet and cobwebby. Almost medieval in its primitive state, it was named for the *Game of Thrones* castle Winterfell. A glossy kitchen wouldn't do here. Instead, the owner, self-professed "lifelong Jewish Anglophile" interior designer Katie Rosenfeld, vowed to keep as much intact as possible—and design the rest of it with a perfectly imperfect spirit. She was going for a certain reaction, she explains: "Wait, was this renovated or not?"

The house originally had a terra-cotta vestibule, but unfortunately it was a bad terra-cotta. Rosenfeld noted that Mediterranean touch that often appears in Tudor-style homes, and she followed the thread and laid the kitchen floor in the material. "Getting it right was a splurge, but it set the tone for the whole kitchen," she says.

An unfitted kitchen was always the plan. "I wanted the room to feel like it was filled with furniture, not big boxy cabinets and built-ins all the way up to the crown molding," she explains. "And I wanted asymmetry." That meant no upper cabinets and making the space room-like and open, despite its petite footprint.

Rosenfeld's work espouses handsome architecture and fine, simple materials in their most natural state (think unlacquered polished brass fittings) and always something a little off, like a single sconce over a piece of found art or a furniture profile seldom seen in a fabric pattern that's hard to place. Feeling fresh within a familiar trope—classic New England decorating—is a feat and a calling card of hers, not to mention the humor. Try not to smile at the collection of Toby jugs grimmacing over at you.

"OUR LARDER IS
like a little curio cabinet
of goodies and food."

Uncommon Kitchens

opposite

Lovingly dubbed "Winterfell" after the *Game of Thrones* castle, this house outside Boston was built in 1926 and revamped by designer Katie Rosenfeld.

opposite

Katie's kitchen obsession manifested her own cabinetry collaboration, Rosenfeld x Bespoke of Winchester, a Boston-area cabinet maker. The paint color is Farrow & Ball Shaded White. The refrigerator is Sub-Zero; the contents are visible, which forces the designer to keep it neat (she likes it that way).

left

The range is the Bussy style from LaCanche; it's petite but gorgeous. The hood inset is from Cove, the hood exterior is wood and custom-made for the space. The larder is to the left.

above

Katie cooks exclusively in Dutch ovens and created several heavy load-bearing drawers exclusively for them. Note that her Le Creuset cookware coordinates with the cabinet color, Farrow & Ball Studio Green. That's dedication.

opposite

English Tudor-style architecture is known for having Mediterranean references—terra-cotta is common. There are eight-inch terra-cotta hex tiles with a smooth finish. The stools are from Noir. The fabric is by Brunschwig & Fils. The over-island light is unlacquered brass and from Visual Comfort.

right

The bar sink that's adorable but never used is made from the same Vermont soapstone as the counters; the faucet and lots of other hardware in the room are polished unlacquered brass in a mix of styles and profiles.

Sounding Off

BIG BUDGET, BIG HOUSE, BIG SPACES: People with big budgets get in the mindset of creating a big space—and then there's a need to justify all the space and so they create storage, and the storage gets filled. But it doesn't have to be that way; you can design efficiently.

ISLAND SEATING: Putting all the stools on one side of the island, I call it "ducks in a row." It's a mistake in function—people need to be able to see each other's faces. They don't want to have coffee with someone next to them. It's not a bar!

ISLANDS IN GENERAL: These are too often a clunky box sitting in the middle of the room. A work table with legs is a bit nostalgic and lighter on the space.

"THE KITCHEN TRIANGLE": The obsession with the kitchen triangle is outdated. That idea of grouping fridge-sink-range is designed for smaller kitchens, but the way many kitchens are built today, it doesn't work. Instead, design in zones. Consider activity spaces: a working or prep space, a secondary clean-up space for sink and dishwasher, and a third spot for serving guests, or even a bar or coffee station.

WHITE KITCHENS: You can create a gorgeous white kitchen, but it needs contrast, like a black hood or something really special. Otherwise, it's a snoozefest. It's the difference between shopping for food at Costco or shopping at a specialty grocer. The former is just big and clinical and empty-feeling.

BIG HARDWARE: It happens too often: hardware that's too big, too square. Too shiny. Brushed. Anything treated and not in its natural state can feel too *fussy*.

opposite

The wall paint is Farrow & Ball Pointing; the trim is Shaded White. The color choices draft off the woodwork and trim paint colors chosen for the rest of the house.

There's no trim on the windows because old English houses with plaster walls didn't have window trim. The sink is a classic fireclay apron-front farm sink from Shaws of England. Most fittings and knobs are brass, but not here—it's a polished nickel faucet. The runner is an antique Heriz.

following pages

The ceramic mugs and pitchers are known as Toby jugs and can depict faces or characters. These are more fun to look at than upper cabinets, thought the owner.

"**A GORGEOUS WHITE** kitchen needs contrast, otherwise it's a snoozefest. It's the difference between shopping for food at Costco or shopping at a speciality grocer. The former is just big and clinical-feeling."

Katie Rosenfeld
designer

NO ONE uses their second sink.

An itty-bitty soapstone sink by the range seemed like a good idea—and it looks great! But that sink gets no use. We don't even fill pots there. Once, my husband tried to wash chicken or something in there and I screamed at him. Why are you washing chicken in my decorative sink?!

You've got to make CONCESSIONS.

Eat-in kitchen or a sitting area? I chose a sitting area. If I had young kids, I probably would have chosen the eat-in kitchen, right? But the kids are grown.

ACCOMMODATE for how you cook.

We cook almost exclusively in Dutch ovens, so my drawers had to hold many, many Le Creuset. No pans, no stainless pots, just those Dutch ovens, so the drawers are quite deep.

On a color journey, look OUTSIDE the kitchen, too.

At first, the kitchen was set to be green—olive—and then perhaps gray or black. But what decided the final color was the beige-white we painted the woodwork in the rest of the house and wanting the crown molding in the kitchen to match that woodwork, so it went from there.

COLOR is more than cabinets or wall paint.

Look around at all the materials. Terra-cotta tile floors and soapstone counters both count as color, and you can work around those.

It's OK to sacrifice storage.

Deciding not to use upper cabinets might screw you for storage but save the spirit of the room. I wanted to look at the Toby jugs rather than upper cabinets that store a bunch of platters. You have to make choices in life!

Come, live the LARDER life.

A small larder—a freestanding pantry—looks like it wouldn't hold a lot, but they're built efficiently, with deep roll-out bins at the bottom. It's like a little curio cabinet of goodies and food. And it makes us not buy more than we need.

People SHY AWAY from glass-front fridges

because you forego the condiments section on the door of the fridge—and you really have to embrace the contents because you see them. But it's great for people who are organized and meticulous, and it forces you to know what's in the fridge and either use it or throw it out.

Not EVERY sacrifice is justifiable.

A lot of my choices were aesthetic over function. I wanted that Lacanche range badly, but I could only fit the smallest size, which meant buying new cookware and revising some of my techniques to use a smaller stove. But it looks so good.

Design for all day and night.

Sconces make it warm and moody and very dim in the kitchen. You have to forage a bit to get around at night, but the atmosphere is beautiful.

CHAPTER 9

Made from Scratch, Known by Heart

The most beautiful part of this kitchen can't be seen—only felt. This room is a love letter to the owner's grandmother, whose rural Louisiana kitchen held dear memories for her. Shavonda Gardner, a designer and content creator, had a very specific, personal kitchen vision, and it revolved around a central table. "A table in the middle of the kitchen is an immediate trigger to gather," she says. And that's exactly what would happen in the small home of her grandmother, where the family would do what you do in a Southern kitchen, she explains: sit and talk, snap beans, shell peas, shuck corn, clean up, and return to the table to eat.

She couldn't imagine it happening at an island. A table is, she says, "the single most inviting nonverbal cue. It signals: Let's talk, eat, drink, be together in the space."

With the core objective—cooking as commune—achieved by floor plan, Shavonda could really flex a decorative muscle. Her jumping-off point was cottage-like English and French kitchens with decorative touches. There's myriad references to these old-world charmers, but executed with deft freshness and more modern materials. For example: In lieu of traditional brick floors, she opted for a brick-style tile with a luxe, glazed finish that's softer on the feet and easier to clean. It's fancier than her grandmother's kitchen but every bit as loved.

Advice on

Materials that age with you

Making it a room

Tapping into sentimentality

opposite

Shavonda Gardner didn't want to "plop a brand-new kitchen" into the 1940s Sacramento, California, house she shares with her partner and two kids, so she chose living materials like soapstone, unlacquered brass, and copper to give it some age. The wallcovering is by Kelly Ventura; it's a custom goldenrod color. The hardware is from Rejuvenation.

right

A rail of copper pots smartly extends over the window to the wall.

Section Two

93

left

Keep your heavy pots
chest-level and close to the
range! This cabinet feels
like freestanding furniture,
which contributes to the
kitchen's room-like quality.

opposite

You can see the slight color
variation from the Ilve
range to the MasterBrand
cabinets; that's by design.
The copper cookware is a
mix of vintage, Rabbit Hill
Copper, and Lagostina.

following page

Shavonda skirted the sink—
it's less monotonous than a
continuous row of cabinets.

"A TABLE IS THE SINGLE MOST
inviting nonverbal cue. It signals:
Let's talk, eat, drink, be together."

Shavonda Gardner

designer *and* content creator

SACRAMENTO, CALIFORNIA

Design it for age, for IMPERFECTION.

The soapstone counters are nearly indestructible, but they get scratches, and that's OK. The materials here are living materials, they're going to look different over time. That's also why we cook with copper pots—a kitchen that feels really used and loved is a happy kitchen.

An island is a work space, a table is COMMUNAL.

An island is for a temporary gathering. It says: Come and sit here while I'm working, but when I'm done we'll get up and go to the table.

Make your guests FEEL something.

A space is working when people walk in and sense the people who live there must have a really cool story. Maybe they feel uneasy or amazing, but everyone feels something.

It's OK to seek a reaction!

I definitely wanted a response from friends, such as, holy crap, that's cool, or, where'd you get that? Or, are your cabinets and stove actually burgundy?!

Look CLOSELY at your inspiration board.

English and French cottage kitchens didn't have islands, and rarely upper cabinets, but they were still functional. Take cues from that.

Hold on tight to what you LOVE.

The idea for the burgundy range and cabinets was pulled from a color in an early Jungalow wallpaper that hung in the laundry room.

ALWAYS choose neutrals for a small space

. . . that's just wrong! I've been fighting against this idea for years, that a small space should adhere to neutrals just to make it look bigger. It's actually easier to commit to a color or pattern in a smaller space; it's a harder commitment when it's expansive, when you could get overwhelmed by it.

FORGET square footage.

Don't give that number so much power! A small space gives so many opportunities. Stop thinking numbers and instead think about the feeling or experience you're going for—not just how to maximize the space.

Be prepared to CHANGE your mind.

I like defined spaces and didn't like the idea of opening up a wall to make this kitchen, but after living there for a while, it made sense because it would afford us the experience I knew we needed. I was resistant to that initially.

Live in your space, LISTEN to it.

Then ask yourself: How can I recreate it in a way that feels natural to the time it was built—and correct for where you or your family is right now? That's how to respect the space and still get what you want.

Matchy-matchy is UNNECESSARY.

The range is one shade of burgundy, the cabinets another. The feeling is monochrome, but the slight difference in hues gives the room depth and impact. People just weren't doing burgundy, but *why not?* I thought!

Section Two

97

CHAPTER 10

A Dated "Builder" Kitchen Beautified

Revamping a
forlorn kitchen

Enlisting
free help

Making it
feel organic

A storybook Victorian on the outside but on the inside, tragically 1980s builder-basic. You know the look: Quality hardwood cabinets but finished in passé yellow lacquered oak. Engineered hardwood floors discolored from wear. Hardware store "feature" lighting. Add forty years and . . . ick.

Meanwhile, all throughout the house was a bevy of fanciful details (oh those theatrical Victorians!). The ambitious designer-DIYer owner had a full renovation in mind for the future, but she set about on an interim kitchen makeover, cherry-picking some of the home's working-kitchen vibes and some niceties, too (brass fittings, painted floors, and ticking stripe curtains—ideas more often seen in the "front of house").

This type of project requires ambition, and without a gratuitous budget it takes patience, too. Owner Jessica Rhodes had both—and conveniently, a family full of skilled, inventive people. To wit: The countertop is actually old pine and maple bowling alley lanes purchased from an online marketplace; her father created a black walnut stain to unify the reddish wood; the planks were stabilized by her engineer brother and then installed by her game-for-anything contractor. Go, team!

Other feats: re-caning the cane-back dining chairs (she learned via video tutorials) and sewing (for the first time) full-length lined curtains. The DIYs began as a way to add beauty to a "functional" interim kitchen, but as the scale and success ratcheted up, so did the family's enjoyment in the space. Here's where they left off.

left

This New York State Victorian came with the name Danascara. Park & Division blogger Jessica Rhodes lives here with her family. Built in 1795, it was remodeled (hello, tower) in 1870 in Italianate style.

opposite

The plate rack trim pattern was cut with a jigsaw to mimic the decorative detail on the old staircase. The antique china is all thrifted or gifted.

previous pages

Upper cabinets were the first thing removed during this renovation—now the room breathes. A mirror makes a good stand-in for a window here. The sconces are from Pottery Barn. The island countertop was a bowling alley lane in a previous life.

left

The original light fixture came with the house—remember to keep what still works.

below

Exposed appliances are unfussy. The fridge and adjacent wall oven and microwave are all Frigidaire. The built-in pantry is practical, but Jessica wishes she added more low drawers elsewhere in the space.

opposite

Since the 1980s cabinetry was quality hardwood, it could be sanded and repainted to feel fresh and new. The basket collection was thrifted over time; the art is by Jessica's uncle Edward Nicosia.

"THIS TYPE OF PROJECT requires ambition, and without a gratuitous budget it takes patience, too. This owner has both—and a creative family to boot."

Uncommon Kitchens

The worn, old floor was vivified with a painted octagon pattern. The designer traced cardboard templates with a pencil and then painted each individually. The project happened over several sessions; she waited for her family to be out of town to finish the final pathways.

Jessica Rhodes
designer *and* blogger

Paint the interior cupboards a CONTRAST COLOR.

You'll be happy every time you open the door, even when it's a mess. It's a feel-good moment without being in your face.

Upper cabinets: TAKE THEM DOWN.

It was the obvious first move. There were uppers over the sink that didn't even reach the ceiling. Taking them down gave the space a room-like feel—it felt freer right away.

Do DRAWERS, not shelves.

It's something everyone tells you to do because low shelves are unloved, accumulate unused things, and are a pain to access.

Visible appliances are HONEST.

Seeing a fridge or a toaster is no different than seeing a TV on the living room wall; it's just the way we live. The utilitarian mixed with the beautiful—that contrast—is what makes it special.

. . . but where you can BE PRETTY, do!

Exposed tools like pots, pans, storage baskets, are useful and a chance to display beautiful objects. You need things like a dustpan and brush anyway, so you might as well get a wood one that's nice to look at.

SUCCESS IS A ROOM you don't want to leave.

Aim for a kitchen where a friend or neighbor or grandmother could come, have tea, and chat with you for hours and hours.

Let paint colors build off the EXISTING PALETTE.

Olive green was the first thought for a cabinet color, but the wood counters have a wink of red in them, and the combination was wrong. Blue was a better playmate for the counters.

Curtains in the kitchen—WHY NOT?

Curtains soften the space, make it feel decorated, and truly give it the feel of a room, not a work space.

PAINTED FLOORS might be what you're missing.

These were a huge decorative stride, and the second they were complete, the room felt done. A pattern sounds like it would feel busy, but seeing it on the floor is a very different experience than staring at it on a wall. It works.

Paint the floor yourself, but BE WARNED.

Do it in sections; leave a path between hotspots like the fridge, sink, and pantry, and try to send the family away for the weekend for the last push. For the intrepid, the formula to DIY painted floors: A de-glosser for treated wood, Kilz oil-based bonding primer, floor paint, and finally, Waterlox sealer.

ID decor clues around the house.

The pattern on the jigsaw plate rail was pulled from a detail on their staircase. Your home offers clues about pattern, proportion, and colors. Repeating those ideas make a new project gel with older parts of the home.

Section Two

107

CHAPTER II

A Mojito Green to Bring It Together

Picture the before: A postage-stamp-size Manhattan apartment. A living-dining-kitchen with one wall of protruding cabinets: dark espresso-finish hulking base cabinets and slick white-lacquer uppers. Eye-catching for sure—and even logical (heft down below and a light-catching material up high). But those boxes bullied the whole room. Designer Casey Kenyon asked the owners to give him two days to scheme up a better way.

The objective, he explained, was to make it feel like one room, not a tiny kitchen and an adjacent space. If anyone could do it, it would be him. Casey's resume is super cool—he worked for renegade designer Paul Fortune in LA, for Marc Jacobs, and for the inventive furniture studio Apparatus. "I'm interested in interiors that are not easily placed in time," he says. One funny trick he uses to hint at agelessness is seen on the sofa: The pillows are understuffed. Modern ones are jam-packed full. Loosen up, pillows, don't try so hard.

Advice on

Bite-size
spaces

Creating an
out-of-time
aesthetic

Occasional
furniture

opposite

In the garden level of a 1910 downtown Manhattan townhouse is this kitchen-dining-sitting room. Nearly all the elements (cabinetry, fireplace, limestone floors) were existing. The upper cabinets were removed in favor of headspace, and the lower cabinets were refreshed with matte paint. Not seen: An integrated Miele dishwasher and Sub-Zero refrigerator.

right

The sofa is the only new item in the room; everything else is vintage. The sofa (by Studio Kenyon Design) and its fabric (Claremont) were picked expressly to feel out-of-time—not exactly vintage, and not new. The counter and backsplash is Caesarstone. The paint color is Farrow & Ball Wimborne White.

Section Two

109

Casey Kenyon
designer

UNIFY with a single color, two materials.

The mint color wraps around the space, hugging it altogether versus presenting a disjointed series of functions (dining, living, cooking). The cabinets are matte paint, the walls are waxed plaster.

The best colors have COMPLEXITY.

Good colors change in the light and have universal desirability. In a bedroom, pale blue is that—but in a public space, a color that can feel saccharine. This green felt not too sweet, not too predictable; it made sense for a space like the kitchen.

Let go of SOME dreams.

The homeowner lobbied for an L-shaped sofa, but it would have cut off the space. The elegant solution is chairs and sofas with ottomans, much more flexible.

Be HYPER specific.

In such a small kitchen, function is key. The ledge above the sink was designed to be just deep enough to place a grocery bag.

Put adjacent rooms to WORK.

Nearby, at the top of the stairs, is an old desk chair that can be carried downstairs to add seating. It was put there intentionally, to be at the ready for when extra bodies are hanging out here. Use the nearby rooms to help your kitchen-dining area grow or shrink as needed.

Form is important but FUNCTION is essential.

Where do you put your keys, your mail, your drink? Occasional furniture, such as a little pedestal table, is important—just drag it where you need it.

Use OLD stuff to make it feel less "catalog."

The modern catalog is an art form, but it's not great for living—it doesn't have soul. Creating the soul or spirit of the place is what home design is about.

opposite

The chest-height wood-burning fireplace posed a challenge—you can't put a sofa or table under it. The fireplace wall has the most special treatment of all, a waxed plaster applied by Kamp Studios. The hairline trim frames the fireplace, making sense of it. The chandelier is by Serge Mouille. The dining chairs are Marcel Breuer Cesca chairs.

Where Flowers Are as Essential as Furniture

First up, let's absolve ourselves of the notion that the sweet styling of this kitchen is artifice. The dried flowers and herbs, the rustic chopping blocks—as it turns out, these are actually the daily artifacts of the owner, a photographer, stylist, home cook, and Canadian nature lover. By displaying these treasures in the most trafficked room in the house, that quotidian cycle of foraging, cooking, and hosting is ever-present. How sweet is that?

The art, the furniture, the sense of place, is all very homey, but it might even be those low 1920s farmhouse ceilings that add the most charm. Low ceilings feel like an impediment to so many home buyers, but that intimacy is a huge asset when creating a convivial room. The intimacy communicates safety and snugness. Add the scent of something yummy roasting and you have a recipe for kitchen perfection.

It's not all quaintness here, of course. The colors here are one-of-a-kind, from the green-leaning stone to the choice of cabinet color. This Ontario country house might just crack open your notion of what's appropriate for a kitchen palette.

left

Nestled in Ontario's idyllic Prince Edward County, this is the 1920s home of photographer Christine Flynn, her partner, two teenagers, and dog.

The antique pine cupboard was the first "sure thing" in the space. Everything else fell into place.

opposite

As a photographer and a sometime shop owner, Christine's styling and merchandising talents are evident throughout the space. Making these "little moments" is just natural to her.

opposite

White is such a common kitchen color, but it's much more effective at feeling fresh when paired with a dazzling dark element, like the honed Verias Green marble here. It's the contrast that makes the impact. (The quirky collections help, too.) The bridge faucet is brass by Perrin & Rowe; the counters are ash.

above

The perimeter counters, backsplash, and display shelf are all the Verias Green marble. The putty pink, Benjamin Moore Cashmere Wrap, is a favorite color, used throughout the home and repeated here.

above

There are tons of charcuterie and cheese boards that get pulled into action when the family hosts friends for get-togethers.

opposite

Art, bottles, dried flowers, rotating shelves of objects—it adds character, points of interest, talking points. Everyone loves the kitchen because there's something to look at.

116

"DRIED FLOWER AND HERBS, rustic chopping blocks—not props but the daily artifacts of this home's creative owner."

left

Christine's own work *Wave #2* hangs. The floors are original to the house; they're pine and were sanded and whitewashed.

below

Chairs from Toronto vintage dealer Guff Furniture surround a Saarinen Tulip table from DWR. The sisal rug is IKEA.

Christine Flynn

photographer

PRINCE EDWARD COUNTY,
ONTARIO

Forget traditional "KITCHEN COLORS."

This is a putty pink we love. It worked in a bedroom, in a bathroom, and now it's on the cabinets. When it works, it works—it doesn't have to be "kitcheny" to make sense.

Compromise yields NEW POSSIBILITIES.

Calacatta marble was the plan all along—creamy white with hints of blush, brown, and gold. But no slabs turned up at the right time. When this Verias Green marble appeared, we went for it. What's unexpected and perfect is how it connects to all the greens and mustard colors throughout the home now.

First love, THEN logic.

The vintage pie cabinet was a piece I'd had my eye on forever at a favorite shop. Once that found a home, the kitchen was configured around it, but even with the new storage, this is still used for entertaining pieces and everyday things. It's wonderful to live alongside the things you love.

The vignettes are CONSTANTLY SWITCHED around.

Some things stay, like the portrait. Others go—the bird is in the parlor now. New flowers come in and dry, old ones go out. The collection of ceramic jugs is ever-evolving, too.

The kitchen collects everyday finds.

The peg board is used to dry and display the things found on dog walks. Lavender, little daisies, furry wheat. The constant foraging keeps the decor constantly fresh.

Without windows, you need SIGHT LINES.

That's why there's no upper cabinets here—any available light from other rooms would have been blocked. Now there are beautiful vantage points all throughout the room and looking into the kitchen, too. It clears space for beauty.

A large island makes the room feel larger!

It's true. We lived with a much smaller island and it wasn't as impactful. The second the larger island appeared, it made the room grander. You only need a corridor of space to move around a kitchen freely—you might as well use the space for impact.

PLAY PRETEND with tape.

Before building the custom island, we marked the floor with tape to practice moving around it and to help visualize the impact of it.

ARCHWAYS offer something special.

First there were doors, then square doorways, and, when the renovation dictated that we were limited to move walls, we decided to add arches instead for a softer flow from room to room—plus it's a nice shape in the mix of straight lines.

Section Two

119

CHAPTER 13

What If It Didn't Look Like a Kitchen?

Advice on

Making dream-
like spaces

Being wrong
on purpose

Emotional
design

Zero surprises that this designer studied cinematography before changing her focus to interior design. Dramatic, photogenic, and memorable is the vibe of Agnes Rudzite, whose projects in her hometown of Riga, Latvia, and worldwide are both brainy and beautiful. Nods to historic European villas and American Case Study houses abound; her references are solidly rooted in future-leaning architecture from the 1920s to 1970s. The firm's kitchens are luxe, no doubt, but in her way of thinking, Agnes offers myriad insights.

opposite

Outside Latvia's capital city, Riga, a kitchen in a 1930s building leans into the period with terrazzo floors. Agnes calls this place a tribute to the iconic Villa Necchi Campiglio in Milan. The apartment has two kitchens; this one's the "social kitchen" as it's exposed to the sitting rooms and is mainly used to prepare drinks and light meals.

Many backsplashes are designed to be, well, splashy. Doing it in glass allows the other elements of the room to take the spotlight. The cabinets are cherry wood.

*left and
following page*

In Moscow, an induction cooktop makes the cooking apparatus super-streamlined, almost invisible in the space, letting the travertine and curvaceous cabinets speak.

120

Agnes Rudzite
designer

Design with your FINGERTIPS.

Consider the sense of touch and color at the same time. Sensual materials like stone and wood, materials that are eternal, that age well, sometimes take a long time to create but are worth it.

There are NO WRONG colors.

All colors are good, it just depends where they appear and in which combination. The space gives you the clues of what color it should be. It could be the location or the view from the window. Something will tell you.

Livable colors LEAN LIGHT.

I am inclined toward paler colors, like sunrise or sunset. Powdery, dusty, pinkish warm hues, or pale blues, like fading sky.

Create SUNSHINE with yellow.

For a space that's quite dark, I'll sometimes give it a yellow, like Farrow & Ball Babouche. And the impression is not that of a room painted yellow, but of a sunlit room.

Good interiors produce EMOTIONS.

You have to feel something when you are inside. There are rooms that are very correct—the colors, the lines—but if it doesn't evoke emotion, it's plain. You have to create the poetry.

PLAYFULNESS is an attitude toward life.

There are so many serious things in the world to worry about. Rooms shouldn't be one of them.

Always have a BALANCE of shapes.

And not just square and linear. Something round. I love when a room doesn't read as very masculine or very feminine, an interior where you can't guess straight away who's living there. If the mood is soft and fluffy and powdery, I'll add something more harsh to balance it.

Get something WRONG.

To achieve playfulness in a space, you need something that doesn't fit in, something off. Think of a beautiful person with everything in place, a god or a goddess. They're intimidating. A small imperfection makes someone even more attractive. It's the same with interiors; you have to make the beauty personal.

We All Love a Vintage Kitchen
(Here's Why)

THERE'S A HUMANNESS TO OLD farmhouse kitchens and English kitchens that modern kitchens just don't have. These older kitchens are typically a collection of objects—items that come and go. Maybe there was an icebox originally and then in came a fridge and it went over in the corner, and then maybe the table was replaced. These rooms have the resonance of time, not the shock of newness nor the stifling uniformity of counters and cabinets installed all at once. Older kitchens are episodic: things were accrued over time and the space evolved for need. It changed as the lives of the people living there changed. And that's what makes it feel so warm— when we sense intimacy, we're sensing that connection between an evolving space and the human experience of evolving.

> We're sensing that the connection between an evolving space and the human experience of evolving.

You can apply some of these to kitchens today. What we do as architects and designers is in part deceit: We're trying to hint at how the space might have evolved over time. We'll ask, what if the family had added a cabinet here and it was a different color. Or maybe they replaced the island countertop at one point. The room comes together as a series of pieces where your eye is reading multiple things together as a montage; there's no monolithic run of upper cabinets or the feeling that it's all one piece. Modern kitchens don't need that relentless sameness of matching cabinets to be successful. It's refreshing for it to feel a little undesigned.

Nate McBride
ARCHITECT

An Austin kitchen lightly renovated by Liz MacPhail; more on page 169.

Section Two

125

(It's the Only Constant)

Leave Space for Change

3

"Did you finish your kitchen?" they'd ask. No. Never! I'd reply in seriousness, because I subscribe to the school that decorating is never done. It's a process, a hobby, a lifestyle! Designer Liz MacPhail put it so well; "Some people work out, some people read, I do house. No one ever says, I'm done with reading, because reading doesn't have a destination or an end goal. It's a passion. And my passion is house."

Not everyone thinks this way, of course. For some, renovating or redecorating is so stressful that the desire to finish the job is palpable. But many of us are well suited to see a room's evolution as just that: a slow-building, growing, and ever-changing experience. Our human needs aren't static, nor is what we need from our surroundings.

The rigidity of kitchen design and its tether to utility is what makes this ethos tough to pull off. You can't move the refrigerator on the same whim you'd move the sofa (Honey, can you pop in for a sec? OK, now grab the other end . . .). That said, back when a refrigerator was an *icebox*, moving it wasn't uncommon at all.

Built-in kitchens only became the norm in the middle of the last century as postwar manufacturing made popular the plug-and-play melamine and chrome kitchen sets. They were cost-effective and quick to install, an all-in-one storage solution. Before that, kitchens were just a collection of furniture, some of which had cooking functions. Before cupboards there was the Hoosier cabinet, an enormous hutch for pantry items and crockery, and prior to that, pans hung on nails hammered into the timber frame or wall. You were typically touching your tools all day—you don't need a drawer for your ladle when its already in your hand. Islands found themselves in the center of the room in the '80s, but the L-shaped counter, a kitchen peninsula, if you will, was the precursor. The sink was once freestanding (see one on page 202), a basin on legs. And a table and chairs, a comfy seat, rugs, art, lamps, and other furnishings made their way in here because there was nothing to say they oughta be stopped. The kitchen is a room like any other.

In the U.K., iconic kitchen designer Johnny Grey has championed the use of "kitchen furniture" to allow for flexibility and comfort. The term used for this approach is unfitted—and there are vocal proponents out there. James Coviello's old-house kitchen didn't come pre-populated with items; he sourced them all, and all of them can be unplugged, or pulled out away from the wall and rearranged. Oh, just imagine the deep-clean you'd enjoy if built-ins were bygones!

"Do you subscribe to the school that decorating is never done? For many of us, it's a process, a hobby, a lifestyle!"

Short of an unfitted kitchen, the looseness, flexibility, and playfulness possible in this room can be achieved by more modest moves. Changing displays of decorative objects, swapping in and out chairs or stools (this is affordable if you thrift shop), adding a lamp to a countertop, removing cabinet doors, tacking up art to a large plain surface, adding table linens or an enormous plant, tossing down a throw rug—these are a few easy ways.

Engaging with your kitchen is the point: Don't let the hulking equipment bully you into thinking you can't have some fun in there. All rooms are living rooms if you treat them that way.

previous

A wild papier-mâché mirror hangs in the LA kitchen of Rhett Baruch, a collector and dealer of contemporary art and design. The resin vessels are by artist Elyse Graham and the cool glassware is by Asp & Hand.

opposite

Scot Meacham Wood's Harlem kitchen—decorated but flexible.

CHAPTER 14

A Brand-New Old Cottage Kitchen

There's a reason they're downright fetishized, those Maine summer houses, those rarified spaces made with run-of-the-mill materials. Spare, singular, and uncommonly welcoming, a quintessential Maine summer place pulls off with head-scratching precision an ambitious melange of unfussy perfection. Its architectural nonchalance is infuriatingly difficult to create today with the character of those built yesterday. Try too hard and you'll flub; it's like stirring a roux or kissing.

Still (like roux and kissing!), it's worth practicing because there's much to enjoy in rooms that don't think highly of themselves. Maybe the volume on everything is turned down a bit and the quality of the company amplified. Maybe weathered work surfaces take the pressure off cleaning. Maybe it's just ineffably charming—soak it in.

This kitchen was born this decade but plays the part of a much older character—and well. The architect reveals all the ways in which he pulled it off with plenty of takeaways for kitchens anywhere, proximity to craggy coastlines not needed.

opposite

On the Maine coast, a series of cabins by architect Nate McBride includes one with this kitchen. Douglas fir counters in the back, zinc on the island for hot pots, and everything within a few steps reach. The central work table is also good for leaning on while chatting with the cook.

above

In one of the three cabins that overlook Penobscot Bay is the so-called kitchen house, one of the structres in the Three Cabins property, was created as open and communal and fit to evolve with the family.

Section Three

131

previous pages

Instead of building one large house, which would have overpowered the landscape, the architect built three cottages, including a kitchen house with an upper loft that's also winterized.

above

Summer cottages are often passed from generation to generation, accumulating pieces and evolving. This one is only a few years old but designed with the same patchwork in mind, which helps it evolve as the family evolves—and looks cute.

opposite

Kitchen furniture, push-in appliances, and a whole bunch of contrasting materials give this space its character. Upper cabinets would have felt heavy and distracted from the view. Lobster pots prompted the open island shelf. The lower cabinets are painted in Benjamin Moore Buckingham Gardens; the ledge is painted Farrow & Ball Cooking Apple Green.

"GET IT ONLY EIGHTY PERCENT done! Don't map out every design detail or furnish it all at once—leave room and time for living in it."

opposite

Art and books go a long way to make a house feel like a home. Don't overthink it, just wedge it where it fits.

above

The good seats at the dining spot look onto the wrap-around deck. The cabinets are painted San Pedro Morning from Benjamin Moore.

Nate McBride

architect

MAINE

It's a ROOM FIRST, a kitchen second.

With a successful design, you don't walk in and say, ah, here is the kitchen, but rather, here is a room I want to be in. There are lots of elements that signal "kitchen." A big one is upper cabinets.

Small kitchens are more EFFICIENT than larger kitchens.

If you truly love cooking, you don't want to move around in a big space; chefs like to have everything they need within a step or two. If you can put that storage elsewhere, you can create an intimate kitchen experience. Large kitchens are part vanity, part excess storage.

If you believe cooking is COMMUNION,

you'll want to be in conversation with whomever else is in the house—not sequestered off. That doesn't mean the island needs a sink or a range, but it does necessitate a place for a non-cook to sit.

An island sink or cooktop can be LIMITING.

The central surface, be it island or table, should be a space where anyone can come and drink, chop, read, just be.

A lesser-used material that works well near a cooktop is ZINC.

You can put a hot pan directly on it. It has a nice patina that feels like it's been with the house for a long time.

Consider WALL-MOUNTED plumbing fixtures.

They save counter space and make sink areas easier to clean.

You don't need a NEW stove to make your day better.

All the product options out there are driven by capitalism, and having to choose between them is just a distraction from life. Purchase an appliance because it's essential to your needs. Avoid thinking about the imagery, what you've seen before, or spending the maximum of what you can afford.

Bottom freezers ONLY!

You can see everything in the freezer when you look down. Freezer on top means you have to bend down to see everything in the fridge!

No granite, PLEASE.

It's the most functional, but aesthetically it has virtually no character. It's uniform and not at all mysterious. And its affordability makes it the go-to choice for developers, so it's everywhere. It's what everyone's kitchen looks like, which means it's not idiosyncratic enough to be *your* stone. Wood countertops need maintenance, but they're warm and accessible.

The TRUTH about design media and social media.

They feature houses, but what we live in are homes. It's architectural pornography: It's sex, not real love.

Section Three

CHAPTER 15

Leave a Little Wiggle Room

Advice on

Designing
one step at
a time

Salvaging
what works

Applying
humor

Can you tell this one was done à la carte? There's the sense here, in the artful mash-up of un-prissy florals and antiques without paperwork, that time has aged this property and that someone young intervened to let in the fresh air.

And indeed, in this one-time chicken coop in Connecticut, the changes happened *petite à petite*, but only over a year and change—just enough time to replace the surfaces, apply a new paint color or two, and swap the furniture a few times.

This one's an argument for iterative design: going slow, embracing the in-between stages, and enjoying the process. And here's the kicker: The homeowner, Robin Henry, is a capital-F fabulous interior designer who has created dozens of magazine-famous kitchens with the requisite level of polish and prestige. But for herself, for her own family, she walked down the path of something more soulful.

There was no singular vision guiding a wham-bam installation like designers know how to do, but Robin's whims, a project done when the spirit moved her. Here, Gaudi tiles and the old pine moldings rub elbows, and chalk paint walls and existing timber ceilings meet cute. The idea wasn't reinvention but just moving the ball forward. And she's not done—might never be. That's the thing about designers, she explains. "Wouldn't it be fun to see . . ." she trails off. "That's the sentiment that drives my kitchen decisions. Some people might see this room as finished, but I'm always thinking about other ways we could do it. Just for fun. Wouldn't it be cool to paint all the cabinets light green, or what if we . . ." This is a kitchen that says: Enjoy the journey.

opposite

The property: An 1835 Connecticut farm. The space: A former chicken coop and root cellar. The visionary: Designer Robin Henry, who lives here with her husband, their two kids, and a dog.

Many different tables have lived here, including one with leaves that expands to host a dozen, but for now, it's a farmhouse table surrounded by vintage rattan bistro chairs and a Swedish sofa with gingham cushions.

"DECORATING IS CREATING
energy in a room. It needs movement,
spontaneity, whims. Perfect rooms
feel like tombs."

Exposed timber, including tree trunks with the bark still on, plus stained pine cabinets—not original to the house, but old—made for a LOT of wood. One wall and the uppers were painted in chalk paint, Aubusson Blue from Annie Sloan, which the designer found to be luminous, not heavy. Atelier Vime makes the rattan lights with colored cord.

Robin Henry worked for the inimitable New York City designer Katie Ridder and remembers an indelible mark during that era: furnishing a petite New York City kitchen with two upholstered chairs, both a terrific luxury and also totally doable in many kitchens, even small ones.

The pet-bowl spout was existing in this kitchen but a novelty worth keeping. Now we all need one, right?

Section Three

143

left

Ranunculus in a vase by
Heidi Lanino. The throw
pillow fabric is by Susan
Deliss.

opposite

The tile below the stained-
pine ledge was the right
move for Robin's family,
but she bets it would be
the first thing ripped out
by a new homeowner. An
inlaid Moroccan table sits
next to a vintage chair. The
decorative plate didn't fit,
but tacking it up to the
wall anyway feels playful
and happy. "Go with your
whims," says Robin.

"**SOME PEOPLE MIGHT SEE** this room as finished, but I'm always thinking about other ways we could do it. What if we…"

opposite

Plenty of designer friends argued for a banquette here, but Robin prefers the flexibility of furniture. Once the sofa was tried out in this space, the family insisted it stay. The chandelier is a Victorian-era rise and fall—that shapely weight assists in raising and lowering the texture.

above

Wall ovens were once dismissed as dating a kitchen, but they're back strong—and chefs have loved and relied on them all along for being ergonomic. The generous pantry affords room for triplicate and quadruplicate snacks.

Section Three

147

opposite

The paint was done bit by bit with no grand plan. Painting the mullions green helped tie in the tile palette. Robin left the rest of the trim as wood—for now. That trim, the walls, and the cabinets are Annie Sloan chalk paint. The trim is Amsterdam Green; the walls are Svenska Blue; the cabinets are Aubusson Blue.

above

The old copper hood came with the house but was installed quite low, at eye level. A real downer! Robin had it reinstalled higher; she says it was one of the best moves she has made. "Matters of scale and placement can be intuitive and are nonnegotiable," she says.

following page

An internet rabbit hole led to these tiles, which were created by Spanish artist/architect Antoni Gaudi for Casa Vicens, a phantasmagoric late-nineteenth-century building—his first-ever commission. The building's exterior was clad in them. Obsessed, the designer contacted the museum and ordered them via the gift shop. Robin likes them, especially because they don't quite reference a specific place or time.

Robin Henry
designer

You don't have to do everything AT ONCE.

If you have the luxury of poking around—starting with one project and moving to another—who knows what will come about? Try something and see how it changes the room. You might keep going or you might pause happily. You don't need a full vision, just a place to start.

Begin with whatever you CAN'T STAND.

For me it was the pink granite counters and backsplash. Even after we removed the backsplash, we had a green drywall backsplash for a year; it was better than bad stone!

Disguises don't work, BE TRUE to your kitchen.

I tried to go all modern in mine. But we live in a barn; it's just not believable. Don't try to make it something it's not; move it forward, make it for today, but don't reinvent it.

GO SLOW, live with the process.

The cabinets were first painted the same pale blue color on the walls, but when it was clear the room could take a deeper, braver color, we changed course. Allow yourself room to experiment in the places you can.

For floors, try CORK.

Cork floor tiles aren't perfect, but they're wonderful. Cork is natural, soft, and warm under your feet. If your floors aren't perfectly smooth, the thin cork surface can be uneven, but it's not bothersome.

Use NON-KITCHEN things.

Not everything needs to be designated a kitchen product. Using furniture meant for other rooms makes it more complicated, more nuanced. It becomes a more interesting place.

Banquettes are LIMITING.

You can use regular furniture in the kitchen. Several designer friends suggested a corner banquette for mine, and it could have been nice. But it's also more limiting and permanent than just using a regular old sofa. When you opt for built-ins, you lose the spontaneity that comes with moving things around.

An "OK" piece is NEVER OK.

If you have an "OK" piece of furniture or element of a room, then it's not beautiful. And if it's not beautiful, it's ugly—it's that simple to me. Of course you can work around items in the house, but be prepared to work extra hard. Or you could take a hard line and say, "Is this beautiful or not?" It simplifies things.

Hardware should be SMALL AND SIMPLE.

Big fussy hardware is unnecessary in a kitchen; ninety-five percent of the time hardware should be a detail, not a focal point.

Decorating is creating ENERGY in a room.

It's not a tableau—you live there, so it needs movement, some spontaneity. You can do that by allowing whims to make it into the design—and then it's OK to change your mind. Perfect rooms feel like tombs.

Section Three

CHAPTER 16

Imperfect Space? Grab the Paint Brush

"My mum brought me up with a bit of the philosophy of: If you feel like a room isn't working, just add another thing. That's how we sort of ended up where we are." This is Brit Eppie Thompson, a crafts entrepreneur known online as The Fabled Thread, which sells cult-favorite embroidery kits to a new generation of fiber art lovers. Eppie calls two kitchens home, the one at her own London flat and one at the family house in Yorkshire.

These two will quicken your pulse either way—for some it'll be love at first sight, for others, it's an art-as-life approach you'd rather visit than inhabit.

Here's what you must know about highly creative kitchens: They rarely look the same for long. Mum is a painter, dad enjoys woodworking, and when Eppie and her sister visit, it's a sewing, painting bonanza. In a wildly artsy household, the only constant is change. Grab your brush.

The look is tailor-made to be additive, inclusive, evolving. There's room for everyone's ideas, and yet nothing is too precious to swap out or update. There's stenciling, hanging art, leaning art, textiles, objects, and yes, somewhere, probably even something to eat.

Advice on

Kitchen as studio

More is more

How to welcome guests

"**THERE'S ROOM** for everyone's ideas, and yet nothing is too precious to swap out or update."

opposite

At the family house in Yorkshire, the kitchen is pink (now), as is the newer addition at rear. The old-house walls are plaster and "about a meter deep," therefore immovable. Instead of renovating, the family decorates.

left

You can watch the weather from a warm and dry perch here in the dining room, which is packed with creative projects—each member of the family is working on something.

opposite

At the family home, everyone wants to sit near the AGA stove (these iron cookers are "on" 24/7), so there's a chair next to it.

right

Back in London in Eppie's own kitchen, the table—for dining but also projects—is purposefully high. High tables are great for cutting fabric, but also chopping. At top you can glimpse part of a PulleyMaid, a hanging wooden clothes dryer. Warm kitchens are traditionally a good place to dry laundry!

155

Eppie Thompson
artist and entrepreneur
LONDON AND YORKSHIRE, U.K.

For cluttered people: SKIP the island.

The more surfaces you have, the more room there is to accumulate clutter. An island didn't work for our family—it was full of rubbish and in the center of the room. With a big dining table, you can push the clutter to one side when you need to use it!

The kitchen table is a CREATIVE hub.

Sewing, crafts, meals, the table is where it happens. It's flexible and used to getting messy, and that's fine. Kitchens are great for making things, and that's not limited to cooking or eating.

LOOSEN UP in here!

With people coming and going and things being taken out and put away, the kitchen is less curated and more flexible than a sitting room. There's a lot that can look and feel right in there. That's the freedom a kitchen offers.

It's EVOLVING.

If you can't get the space right, focus on what you can control—colors and objects—and keep decorating. The idea being: The spirit of the kitchen is ever-changing.

BENCHES, not chairs, for a small household.

You don't need loads of chairs if you're just one or two people. Have at least one bench—it can accommodate multiple people, but it can be tucked in when not in use.

White cabinets are in stock and CHEAPER.

But they don't have to stay white! In London, mine are painted with a primer meant to coat the laminate exteriors (such as Zinsser BIN), and then a hard-wearing latex paint color-matched to an iconic India yellow. And there are new handles. The colored cabinets were too pricey; this was a way around it.

If you want more time TOGETHER,

make a welcoming kitchen. People will hang out there while you cook. Make it a place you all really want to be.

Counter-height work tables SOLVE problems.

A high table is a good project table (for cutting and sewing and also food prep).

A rug tells you to sit and STAY a while.

At my mum's, everyone wants to sit near the warm AGA cooker. The chair and the rug nearby tells them they're welcome to do that. You don't want to sit in a place that feels like someone is going to wipe up before and after you!

Textiles in the kitchen—it's OK!

A rug in the kitchen means you're a little more careful about not spilling. You won't put your best rug in there, but I've never had a problem with rugs or cushions or even embroidery art that couldn't be easily remedied. It adds a level of comfort that's hard to match.

Section Three

157

Extraordinarily Commonplace, Universally Special, a Room for Everything

IT'S ABOUT SO MUCH MORE THAN COOKING.

If you've ever attempted to nudge your guests from standing around the kitchen to sitting in one of the "nicer" rooms of the house, you've seen this room's magnetic pull at play. This isn't just where people gravitate, it's home away from home.

> "They say hell is other people's dishwasher-loading techniques."

The kitchen is a dazzling paradox. It's wonderfully universal; most are arranged intuitively—it would only take you a few tries to find a water glass in a stranger's kitchen. But it's also deeply personal: they say hell is other people's dishwasher-loading techniques.

And in a family kitchen, where there's no single author of the space, the alchemy is magnified. This is a collaborative performance art project, whether you like it or not.

Food comes in, refuse goes out, it's never static, never the same room twice. This space does more living than the living room. And there's almost no activity that doesn't make sense inside these walls. Repot plants; use bleach or tie-dye; do homework. Pay bills, make calls, do something crafty. Is it messy? Take it to the kitchen, please!

If you're visiting someone for the first time, watch yourself naturally linger there. You're not going to gaff in the kitchen. There's no wrong chair to sit in, no breakable heirlooms. You know exactly how to be there.

You can entertain a toddler here with a drawer of plastic containers or wooden spoons and pots; you can sit across the table or lean against the perimeter with anyone—a client, a contractor, a member of the clergy. This is almost always the right spot to do it. It's safe, it's neutral. Need to have a difficult chat? Want to fight? Looking for a place to blow out the candles and dole out cake? Kitchen.

Universal, predictable, indestructible—plus a hearth, and often, cookies. What's not to love?

Uncommon Kitchens

opposite

Red glass hardware, stained glass, and oil paintings make a kitchen by Geremia Design special.

A Pantry That's a Bureau, Too

Here's a modern concept for you: A family combines two apartments in an LA duplex. Some seasons they splinter off the top unit as a guest suite or vacation rental; sometimes they need it big (gang's all here!). The two full kitchens seemed unnecessary, but a second place to make a bite to eat can be useful—at least sometimes—so what to do?

The genius solution by designer Laurel Consuelo Broughton was two-fold: a push-in stove that can be stored and replaced with a cabinet. And an adjacent storage unit—truly just drawers and shelves behind doors—works as a pantry or for clothes storage. A great place for snacks . . . or balled-up socks!

The resulting space is multifunctional, not at all redundant with the primary apartment, and expands and contracts as needed.

above

Dubbed the Yolk House for the brazen yellow staircase, this 1939 Spanish revival in the Echo Park neighborhood of Los Angeles is a sweet duplex apartment, now combined. The paints are all Benjamin Moore: the kitchen walls are Sun Washed, the ceiling is Peach Cloud; the walls with arches are Mayonnaise, a cult favorite.

opposite

The stairway to the second floor is painted a Benjamin Moore color called Bold Yellow, go figure. Designer and homeowner Lauren says it makes the whole passageway glow.

previous pages

The designer-homeowner worked with Formica to create a custom-made kitchen unit. The stove is often pulled out, stored in the garage, and replaced with a cabinet when more living storage is needed.

left

The unit to the right was built to be multifunctional; it can be a pantry or, when the space isn't utilized as a kitchen, the cabinet can hold linens and clothes.

below

This table and bench were built for the space. The floors are linoleum.

opposite

The arch was added between the two rooms; it echoes the arched cut-out in the wall. The wall sconce by the window arch is Commune. The pendant over the table is by Muuto.

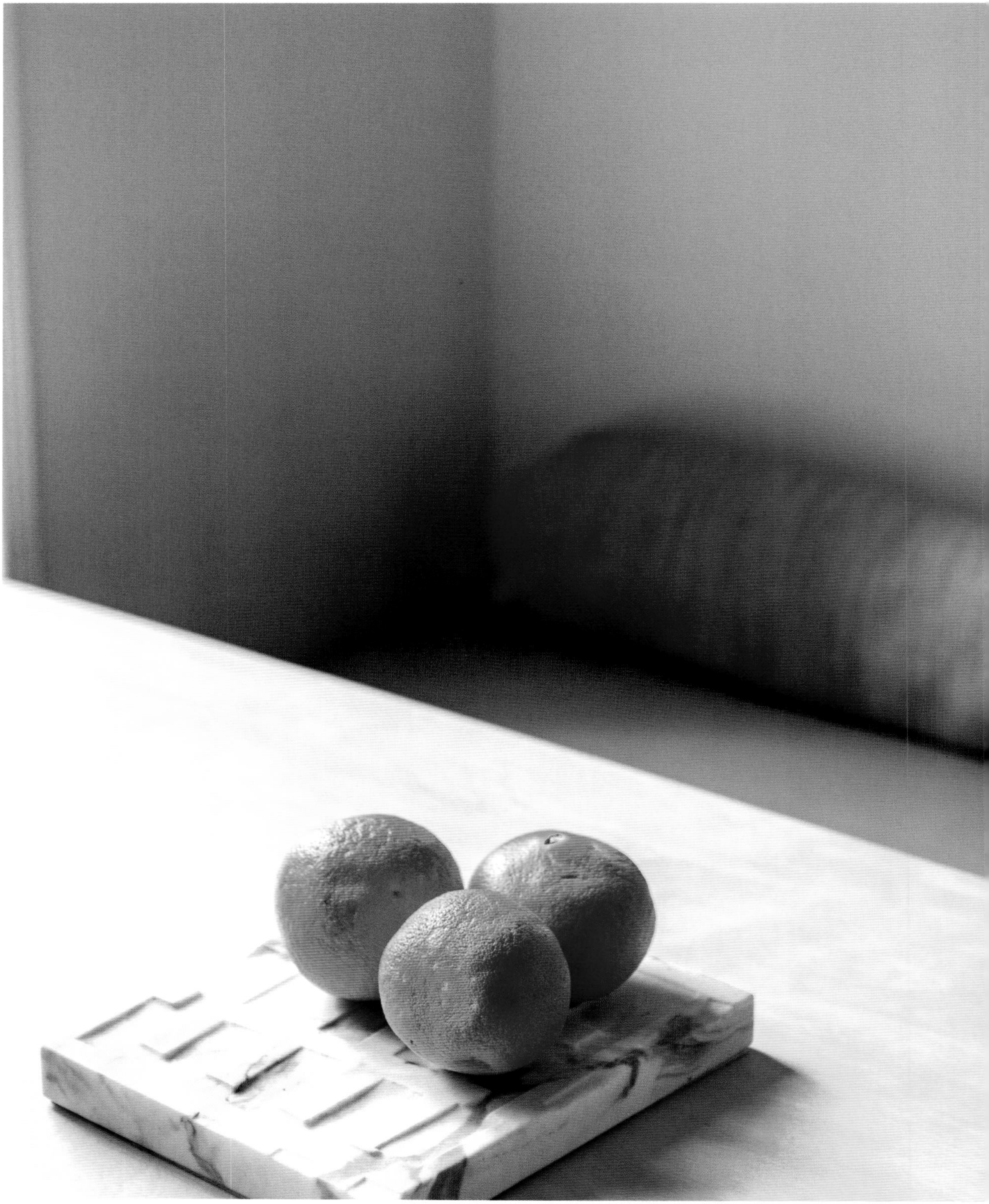

Laurel Consuelo Broughton
designer

Create your own WARM light.

Paint colors and light work together to create feeling or mood in a room. And there are colors that mimic warm light, such as peach or yellow.

To add ENERGY, use two paint colors.

Try two similar but different paint colors on opposing walls to add interest to a space. Two tones of peachy pink here play up how the light moves around space. The lighter and darker tones work off each other.

New houses need old-house TRICKS.

Green is the theme in this space, but the green vintage bathroom sink, green tile, and green Formica cabinets don't match per se—and that's intentional. It makes it come off a little less "planned." The idea is to let the different materials be themselves and to not be too color coordinated, just the way matching shoes and a blouse would be a bit dorky.

You can reapply HISTORY to a building.

Old homes have little repairs that don't quite match. Newer homes obliterate that. There's an intentional pink "repair" tile on the green floor; it reminds us of what came before and what exists now.

Materials choices: Sometimes you just KNOW.

I grew up with black-and-white check floors; we installed them here. I knew all along that I wanted that. Setting them diagonally instead of straight along the walls gives the classic material a more modern feel.

Let the use inform the COLOR.

This room is sometimes not a kitchen, and the palette reflects that—these peaches and greens are almost like bedroom colors, something you don't expect from a kitchen, which makes sense because we're trying something unique.

Section Three

167

CHAPTER 18

Very Vintage, No Dishwasher, No Apologies

What would your kitchen look like if it was used only part-time? That's the freedom this one presents—it's the kitchen of an Austin, Texas, design firm, used primarily for warming up lunches, hosting small industry get-togethers, and the impromptu chats that are native to this room.

The beauty here is in deciphering which parts of the room are original to the house and which were lovingly restored or added fresh by interior designer Liz MacPhail. The color story—none vintage, all new—took shape beginning with the linoleum tiles. Hers is a technique lots of designers use: Begin by choosing the material with the smallest palette. Pick the best (or least offensive) option and build from there. These Forbo tiles are offered in only a handful of colors (oxblood red it is) and the rest of it just fell in line, not a lot of overthinking involved.

As it turns out, only the wood base cabinets and hulking-but-sensuous O'Keefe and Merritt stove came with the place (though not in working order). But the linoleum tiles are new, and the glass-front cabinets are, too—custom-made for the space. Other updates are minimal, functional even, but the room doesn't demand much—it's already convivial and beautiful, exactly as intended.

Advice on

Analog living

Strange color victories

What to heave and what to keep

opposite

This Austin, Texas, bungalow is the design firm of Liz MacPhail. The workhorse 1950s Youngstown iron double sink was resurfaced by a pro. The ribbed washboard on this side is for letting clean dishes drip dry. The dining table was found at a yard sale in the neighborhood; the metal stools are also vintage finds. The new Smeg twenty-four-inch fridge was bought to stay in keeping with the kitchen vibe; it's retro in feeling but has utilitarian bottom freezer drawers.

left

A lover of old houses, Liz was partially inspired to purchase it in order to preserve it.

Section Three

169

Uncommon Kitchens

"SOME PEOPLE EXERCISE OR READ OR TRAVEL, but 'house' is also a hobby—and it's never done. No one ever says, OK, I'm done reading. If it's a passion, you're constantly doing it; there's no destination, no end goal."

opposite

The new, custom upper cabinets in stained wood and glass were added to elevate the cabinetry and tie together the style of the kitchen with the home's existing dark-stained millwork and trim.

above

The O'Keefe and Merritt stove is original and was kept in place for its charm. It's an approximately $5,000 repair job away from simmering a soup. Still, it's pretty. The oil-on-canvas painting above the bar cart is vintage, found on eBay.

Ask, *What can WE KEEP?*

People go around renovations the wrong way—they instinctively look for what they want to change. Instead, ask what's worth salvaging, restoring, or keeping and moving to another room.

Add ONLY what's necessary.

Don't subscribe to "musts"—your rooms need only what they need. Here, we needed a garbage disposal—no one ever volunteers to clean the drain catch—but not a working stove because it's an office. There's a new, conventional plug-in refrigerator, but no ice machine because it wasn't one hundred percent necessary; we can make ice!

"Use it up, wear it out, make it do, or do WITHOUT."

The famous World War II slogan was top-of-mind here. The cabinets were kept and painted, the interiors wallpapered. The glass fronts were added to increase the feeling of openness.

Give it one SLIGHT TWIST.

Start with a classic: a checkerboard floor. The expectation is iconic black and white, but black and red, a nontraditional approach, is a safe way to have a little bit of fun.

Skip big-box shopping—go THRIFTING.

You can outfit the kitchen with matching glass and china from a big-box store, or you can, for the same price, shop vintage sellers or eBay for pieces that make dining special and dishes joyful.

Not everything is a design STATEMENT.

Even beautifully designed rooms have spots for the eyes to rest. There are main characters and supporting cast—not everything needs to have a strong point of view.

When people question you, you're onto SOMETHING.

The most personal choices, the ones you'll love living with, often aren't right for others. So don't be offended if someone questions your choices—it might mean you're onto something good.

A TABLE is an island and more.

A table in the kitchen gives you that thing we all want: a connection to the kitchen as a social gathering place. The kitchen does bring us together, whether it's for cooking or doing homework with your kids. And there's an intimacy to a dining table that works for all this.

Using special things makes it SPECIAL.

Things don't have to be precious or expensive to be special. At the office we use Depression glass tumblers, classic English patterned plates that are burgundy, and utensils that are brass with wood handles found at a secondhand store.

NO ISLANDS, Thanks.

I don't like sitting at an island to eat. Counter stools are functional and convenient for informal dining, like for breakfast or for a drink. But I think we've gone too far on the kitchen island.

Section Three

The Kitchen Ever-Changing

THERE'S A GRAND BUT HOMEY, *charming, and beguiling kitchen in the U.K. that has come to represent all that's good and right and possible in this room. It's both historic and forward-looking, "done"-feeling and flexible. It's decorated the way an "unkitchen" often is, uninterested in architectural backflips and veering away from conventional beauty. It has been with and without rugs, painted white and green, and then green and red, and still, its owner is tinkering. Here are a few tidbits from a conversation with the room's author, architect George Saumarez Smith.*

I've been brought up with the idea—it's ingrained in British culture—that you can do things in an amateur way. While continental Europe likes bureaucracy and professionalism, the English submit to the idea of a gentleman-amateur. I'm a professional architect, yes, but not a decorator or designer.

I once did a talk around the time my home was published in a magazine, and a woman asked: How do you choose fabric for the cushions, and all I remember thinking was, who cares! As an architect, we think a lot about how, for example, molding finishes a room; those things are important to us. But the colors in my kitchen, the cushions . . . it doesn't really matter; it's not going to ruin my day if the colors are not exactly right.

And the colors are not exactly right! I've always loved deep red. It's hard to find a paint with the amount of pigment you need to pull this off; the one I used here, from Papers and Paints, works. The green one, though, isn't exactly what I had in mind. It's a lot more green than the blue-green I expected, and Christmas tree green is my least

above

An earlier version of the kitchen—sans rugs and with white cupboards that George designed. The wall-length one on the right stores crockery and pantry items but also household filing and other household storage, including, funnily, a lot of CDs. On the range side is a panelled fridge, freezer, dishwasher, waste bins, and drawers. Appliances are plugged in and hidden on that side, too.

right

The current state of the kitchen has contrasting cabinet colors and rugs. The central feature, a now-discontinued island and washstand from Bulthaup, remains.

favorite color. But once it was painted I decided that I'll live with it for a while. A friend said, oh, it's like port and starboard. And I guess it is.

English taste likes things that are a bit soft around the edges, a little worn; we like things that are not too new. That immediately conjures up a feeling. Something "comfortable" is almost never expensive or brand-new.

The legacy of the British Commonwealth is that it was so far-reaching, the colonies stretched all over the world, and so the DNA of an English home is in part bringing things back from travels. Plates and Delftware, rugs from Morocco.

My house is unconsciously arranged, but the downstairs is the most old-fashioned; the top is modern and the middle is a blend of the two. The inherited furniture doesn't mix that well with modern things. If you've got a mix, you've got to tune the dials differently, hence using the different floors to create the right mix.

Everyone loves the rugs in the kitchen, but they were sort of an accident. There were several kilims and old rugs in the basement that were soaked in a flood, and I brought them up to the kitchen to dry. It's always warm in the kitchen, the AGA keeps it so. And they just stayed.

George Saumarez Smith,
ARCHITECT

"My kitchen forces me to be tidy. This is a kitchen that only works if you put everything away," says George. "It's a room for one person and one helper, and the storage is a 3D jigsaw puzzle and I'm the one who knows where everything goes."

Do This Instead

Forget the Gut Reno...

4

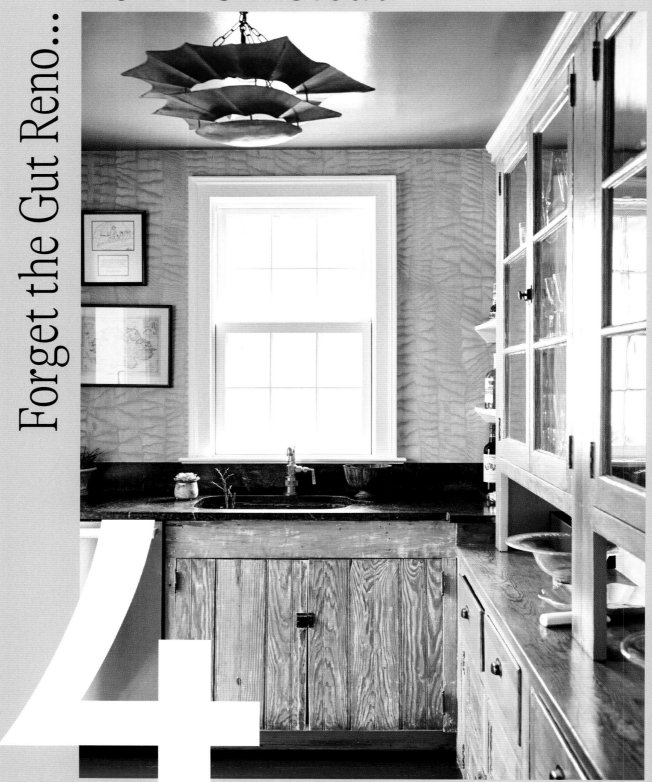

There's a wild contradiction held by home-lovers out there: the quest for a charming apartment or house, something with character, and then the thirst for an absolutely unsparing gut renovation.

Sometime in the 2000s, it felt like the American dream shifted from single-family home ownership (house, yard, fence!) to all that plus a wrecking ball. House and garden TV shows seemed to fuel our collective impulse. The ratings spoke: The more sledgehammers per segment, the more male viewers tuned in. The model was: *He* demos, *she* decorates. (I know, right?) It's easy to knock, but who doesn't love a before-and-after?

But hold up! Those old-home ineffable charms often don't survive a to-the-studs renovation. Think about it: You can't expect to clearcut a forest in February and see bunnies back by May. A more sensitive approach is in order—weed out the dying timber to allow for sunlight, and leave the rest alone; call it the kitchen ecosystem.

Memorable kitchens are rarely from scratch; instead, they cherry-pick moments of integrity, or at least utility, and layer in eye-catching or of-the-moment . . . *moments*. And this is where kitchens designed on a budget succeed over their big-bucks brethren. Out of necessity, a budgeted kitchen requires keeping the passable parts: the footprint of the space, a wonky island, or all the cabinetry, scummy as it may be (paint helps!). But it also requires deft design work, decorative distractions, or other ingenious solutions that mix existing materials with the new. It's that mix that's magic, it's restrictions

In an early 1800s Greenwich farmhouse, designer Libby Cameron kept the original cabinetry. The wallpaper is Sarkos, the ceiling color is Parma Gray by Farrow & Ball. The light is by Circa Lighting.

that invite invention. Watch designer Meta Coleman prove this in brave new ways on page 208.

The truth is, your old house or even your dated house holds answers to your newly refreshed, livable, lovable house. If the space was built with a modicum of integrity, then there are cues in terms of scale and use of space that are worth holding on to.

A light-touch renovation—think scalpel, not sledgehammer—is not only the more environmentally responsible choice (construction waste accounts for nearly half of landfill content worldwide—gross), but it makes the impending design choices remarkably easier.

Your current kitchen space offers a trail of bread crumbs to a successful refresh, you just have to look for them.

The converse is also true, and I've lived it. The home we bought had a kitchen most would call dated—white slab-front cabinets, turquoise walls, melamine counters and a workhorse stove straight outta *Leave It to Beaver*, or so I'm told. To repair the electrical meant taking it down to the studs, and it was decided the cabinets weren't strong enough to be remounted.

> There's a subtle narration communicated by aged things: I've made it this far. And that bodes a feeling of trust.

When demo was done, the white drywall box meant I was starting from scratch—and it would take more than colorful cabinets and a rug to warm it up. Keeping the old counter or existing cabinets would have offered a starting place, something to work around at least. (More about my own place is on page 247.)

That's the thing about demolition: It's faster and cheaper for the crew to really whoop it up and bring it down to the studs than it is for them to leave specific vestiges of the old place. Demo is a fast-moving train.

Stop and consider what you have going for you—every challenge presents an opportunity. Low ceilings bode intimacy and cozy feelings. Worn surfaces feel loved. A dark room can make bold colors feel mellow and welcoming. Dated appliances can last longer and work better than the new ones. (Your parents were right.) Lemons > lemonade, folks.

And if you're staring at a delectably flawed 1990s construction with wacky proportions and a harebrained floor plan, you're excused! Ignore the architectural cues and create a happy place within it. Here's where old things and antiques can really help—they add instant patina, immediate warmth. The idea is to direct the eye away from the passé.

opposite

A few eighteenth-century flourishes remain—with some that were added—in the Catskills, New York, kitchen of James Gardner.

There's a subtle narration communicated by aged things: I've made it this far. And that bodes in us a feeling of trust. If those don't work for you, maybe this old adage will: Never let the oldest thing in the room be you.

A Cabin Charmer Served à la Carte

Advice on

Thinking
like a chef

Displaying
your stuff

Marrying decor
and function

The feeling of love comes across strongly here. And that's not a look you can style your way into; it's a feeling that happens in rooms where love is made—loving the rituals of cooking, loving the energy of a good dinner party, loving one another even when something gets burned. In this kitchen the good china is used, the oven's turned up hot, things get messy, and friends stay until the dishes are done.

There are decorated kitchens and there are chef's kitchens. This one is both—a pleasure to cook in and a delight to visit—picture this jubilant space with the smell of something yummy and good tunes and cute people. Nice, right?

Plentiful stuff—pots, lamps, books—helps this room spill into the next. The pieced-together aesthetic is right for the setting, a summer community of old camps just north of New York City. The cabin interiors are still pretty rustic, so when the kitchen was renovated, it wasn't toyed with so much that it felt out of sync. The previous incarnation had "cheddar cheese"–colored walls, and those stayed; the Moroccan tiles arrived because the couple has a home in Tangier. They decided on green because it seemed a fun accompaniment to the orange walls. Why not?

Uncommon Kitchens

left

In an old cabin community in Upstate New York is this cutie of a hideout, the home of Rob Ashford, a Tony and Emmy Award–winning director and choreographer, and Kevin Ryan of A-list landscape firm Madison Cox Associates. Stone stairs and a rustic garden fence welcome guests.

opposite

The original kitchen was tiny, as all the meals were taken at the resort's clubhouse. The range and hood are Wolf; the fridge (a sliver at far left) is Sub-Zero. Moroccan tiles create the backsplash; the rug is from Tangier. The china and pottery collections are the couple's pride and joy. They're used often.

opposite

A dining room just off the kitchen is filled with the couple's treasures. The collection of Blue Willow china began with pieces handed down from Ashford's grandmother; they grew it by purchasing more at auction.

right

The French school chairs were spotted at a shop in London, snoozed on for years, and refound once the couple had a home for them. Narrow dining tables (this one's from Thailand) make for lively dinner parties—it keeps conversation intimate and flowing.

"HERE, THE GOOD CHINA IS used, the oven's turned up hot, things get messy, and friends stay until the dishes are done."

above

The screened-in porch is a newer addition to the old home. Ryan painted the floors, with advice from their friend designer Gene Meyer—the homeowner chose fifty possible colors, and Meyer came with the final picks and plan.

Rob Ashford
choreographer *and* producer

Kevin Ryan
design exec

Entering a GOOD kitchen

is like walking into someone's comforting arms. When the house glows, it has a pleasant aroma, when the atmosphere is welcoming and warm . . . that's what you aim for.

The JOY of collecting dishes

is the gratification you feel when you pull out the right one for the meal. Our dishes were collected from around the world—Italy, England, Morocco. And the meal gets a nice lift from interesting china; everyone notices!

Open shelves work for PRACTICALITY and joy.

You can see what you own and you can also easily ask guests to help out—"hey, will you pass that green bowl?" Plus, when you own things you love, it's nice to see them and be reminded of how they came to you.

Open-shelf maintenance—it's NOT hard.

A workhorse exhaust hood keeps grease out of our kitchen. And if you really use your dishes, they won't collect dust or scum. We wipe down the shelves maybe twice a year.

Major cooks need major HOODS.

If you want to sear, to fry, to cook at high heat, you want the smoke and odors to be pulled out, and that requires a powerful hood. This hood is not for show—it's not a statement piece like in some kitchens—it's there to do its job.

EDIT your belongings for the space you have.

Here there was only a narrow space for a fridge-freezer. We figured, better to unbundle it; so we have a tall thin fridge and a separate freezer drawer, and we're able to use every inch to its best ability.

Lamps are warm and HOMEY.

Even in this small kitchen, there are two lamps. They're the first on in the evening and the last off. After the room is cleaned and everything's put away, it feels so inviting to go back into the lamplight to get a glass of water or something. It's a very different feeling than an overhead light.

WHY linoleum?

The kitchen floor is a deep purple-blue linoleum, which is great for a chef because you're not standing on a hard surface, and you don't need one of those rubber cushions either. Tile would shatter dropped dishes—and we love our dishes!

It's only TIME for a new kitchen

when you've exhausted all your options. If you've lived there for years and been creative with your choices and you still say, there's more I want to do here, then it's time to play with a new set of options.

Section Four

189

CHAPTER 20

Just Enough New

Rolling with a home's imperfections is one of the greatest signs of a confident design lover. To eschew the fight for perfection and to embrace the weird and unruly, even play along with it, means you're not impeded by the oddity but adorned by it. It's defiant and bold and quite frankly, pretty badass.

There's a kitchen in Tennessee by powerhouse designer Rodman Primack that espouses this POV and is as startlingly cool for what it isn't as for what it is. All around the house is fabulous art (the passion of the home-owners) and groovy commissioned furniture. Who would've thought this same family would OK leaving the existing kitchen cabinets in place versus going whole hog on a revamp?

Rodman and his clients are among that choice group of folks who look for what's worth keeping in a redo. Now here's the real flex: The firm showed its aesthetic acumen by accepting the not-so-special cabinets and directing the eye hither and fro with the bold cement tiles' ingenious colorblocking. See how it breaks up the white boxes and dances the eye around the room?

Truly deft design work trusts itself, comes in under budget once in a while, and never takes itself too seriously. This Tennessee family was an A-plus collaborator, but it's fun to hear Rodman playfully snipe at design lovers who are woefully caught up in the current state of over-the-top kitchening we've found ourselves in. There's a serious knowledge drop in this farmhouse, so take note.

Advice on

Budget buys
made brilliant

Getting
your values
straight

Accepting
the imperfect

opposite

In Tennessee horse country is a farmhouse kitchen that wasn't overworked during its renovation. The varying styles and colors—the vintage French lighting (the sconces are Jieldé), orange Bertazzoni stove, and Mexican cement tiles in a creative color-block pattern—are a nod to the Blooomsbury Group style of living and decorating. The white cabinets were simply refreshed with paint. The red lights were designed by the firm and produced by Shelton Studios in Brooklyn.

following pages

A table with leaves can be pulled out and expanded for a crowd or tucked neatly against the island, as it is here. There's a bit of Shaker influence here, a nod to the local community.

Section Four

Sounding Off

THE LATE-CAPITALIST TENDENCY
TO OVER-ANTICIPATE COMFORT

There's a real obsession out there with the idea of having everything—with being able to say: We have it all covered! Eight counter stools is definitely something people ask from our firm. But I've never seen eight people sitting on counter stools at a kitchen island. There could be six or eight people right in the kitchen during a party; but only three at most on stools, perhaps one person standing next to them, two over here, one preparing food. They're certainly not all on stools staring at the host doing dishes or making dinner.

I think we often overthink the possibility of someone's discomfort. We're obsessed with quantifying how much of each thing we might need to be comfortable. Weirdly, in Europe and in England, there's much less attention to meeting people's needs, and yet the homes are super-comfortable. Because it's not about ensuring that everybody has the same seat. So what if not everyone fits? Well, you'll pull in a chair from the dining room. Oh, but that's so annoying, they'll say. But it's really not, and adding that other seat, a chair instead of a stool, means the room feels less like a catalog or a hotel. The space seems immediately more real.

Sometimes the job of a designer is the job of saying no, you don't need eight counter stools. To keep them from their desires and realign them with what they value, which is having a welcoming space.

—*Rodman Primack*

A 1930s cantilevered armchair by Alvar Aalto was placed beside the Rais stove to make the kitchen a welcoming spot, even when food isn't the objective. The art is *Cowhide/Fried Egg* by Math Bass.

195

"**TRULY DEFT DESIGN WORK**
trusts itself, comes in under
budget once in a while, and
never takes itself too seriously."

A view of the Arts and
Crafts house decorated
by New York firm RP Miller.
"We were happy to keep a
few things that didn't work
perfectly," Rodman says.
"That's why it feels so cozy
and out of time."

Rodman Primack
designer
TENNESSEE

To make a big kitchen inviting, try a table with LEAVES.

They expand and contract depending on who is home that weekend. A kitchen won't feel lonely when the table is made small—and it can be pulled out and expanded to fit a group if lots of people are visiting.

A kitchen must be inviting at ALL times.

Old homes often have kitchens away from the action, that's why there's a stove and a chair here. This one doesn't overflow into entertaining rooms; it's by itself, so it needs to be an inviting destination by itself.

The fun part of design is making it work . . . even when it's not IDEAL.

We're too lazy! Materials are so available now; we have so many choices, it's so easy to say, oh, just tear it out. But if the kitchen works well, I'd much rather you buy a painting with that money.

Calibrate your desires with your VALUES.

If cooking isn't a major part of your life, spend your money elsewhere than on the range; spend it where you value it. You might not need twenty burners, only six burners. Get yourself to a clear place about need, not fantasy.

The kitchen can be centering and GROUNDING.

Growing up, a lot of what happened in my life happened at the kitchen table. I want to create that space for my clients' families, too.

Let PURPOSE drive the material.

Chopping a lot? Do a butcher block counter. Stainless steel is good because you can use it, beat it up, and it still looks good. Avoid materials that are hard to work with and hard to replace. Your kitchen shouldn't drive you crazy.

A cotton rag rug is COZY and NICE.

Wash it for years and when it's worn, replace it.

MINIMIZE the number of materials you use.

You don't need forty different materials and details; you can mellow it down to a few special materials. Don't fall into the trap that, because you can afford it, you should do it.

There are FRESH options for backsplashes.

Wood can work—it looks good stained, it's beautiful in old Mexican kitchens. And cement tiles are so matte they almost mimic plaster. Think beyond glossy tile.

Hardware DOESN'T need to be STANDOUT.

There's thinking that the hardware has to be "the jewelry" of the room, but it doesn't. It can be quiet or go away, and other things can be loud.

Families that love to eat and enjoy HOSTING deserve beautiful dishes and glasses.

We sometimes commission the creation of those items, investing the time into creating something special, but even collecting those items is wonderful because that's a category of decoration that's not easily damaged by daily use, and it makes the lives of the users more special.

Section Four

197

This Old House (Prefers New Appliances)

Advice on

Salvage made
functional

Taking your
sweet time

Integrity, no
matter what

A period piece this is not. Don't expect a gentleman with a twisted mustache and a vintage timepiece to step out from this riff on an early nineteenth-century kitchen; in fact, the owner is a fashion person; think: good jeans and a perfect navy sweater. Thoughtful, unfussy. That sort of approach to style tracks here in the kitchen, too—don't mess with the classics.

The takeaway of this Upstate New York kitchen is this: Solid wood furniture with quality hardware is, well, nicer than MDF cabinets. Glass mason jars are more comely and just as airtight as vacuum-sealed plastic vessels, and china and flatware tarnish and break, so you might as well enjoy the stuff that comes with a little soul.

But this isn't a purist's kitchen. The appliances are new because the owner, James Coviello, is a real chef. He prepped and cooked and hosted in this petite kitchen—the onetime outbuilding of this 1864 house—for more than a decade before finally renovating it. (Yes, these are the "afters.") As he was a stickler for integrity, the criteria for choosing appliances weighted performance more heavily than aesthetics—and that mix of no-nonsense stainless steel tools with wonky cupboards and tooth-by-jowl furnishing is the charm. It has throwback elements, but it's not a costume drama.

left

As is true with many old houses, the kitchen of this 1864 Greek Revival country house in Upstate New York is an addition; some were even separate buildings to ensure safety if the structure were to catch fire. Practical!

opposite

Fashion designer–turned–interiors and homewares designer James Coviello lived with a gross 1980s kitchen for many years before turning back the clock on the room. Nearly everything here was found, salvaged, or built for the space; good new appliances were essential as he cooks. (This is a Fisher & Paykel fridge with bottom freezer.)

left

The collection of vases are known as Old Paris Porcelain and date between 1860 and 1900. They were made in France and were imported to the States, becoming popular in the South. Coviello found his first one in Bangkok, improbably, and then added to the collection.

above and opposite

The butler's pantry hutch is a nineteenth-century country cabinet bought locally; it kept its original paint. The rest of the built-in shelving was existing and repainted.

above

Old sinks, new faucets. Coviello swears by the brand Strom Living, which offers vintage-style profiles. The 1930s farmhouse sink with legs was found on eBay; he drove to rural Pennsylvania to retrieve it. The counter is a reclaimed nineteenth-century marble table top mounted on large vintage sink brackets.

opposite

The original nineteenth-century painted wood floor was hidden below five layers of linoleum and plywood stacked up over one hundred years. Coviello removed the layers, scrubbed the floor, and polished it with clear Briwax furniture wax.

opposite

The range is a De Longhi thirty-six-inch professional style gas double oven; the hood is XO brand. The overhead light was found at a big-box furniture store—always worth a look, he says.

above

In the dining room, cool finds, mostly from Asia, line the top of a mantel, old and wooden, but faux—there's no firebox here.

James Coviello

Autopilot renovations are a DISASTER.

You'll visit a house and get a tour and the host will say, "Well, the kitchen was redone in 1997, so it's due for an update!" But why? Does it need to be updated, or can just the appliances be updated? So many kitchens are built in a way that, if you touch one thing, you have to touch everything, but that doesn't have to be. You can make incremental improvements.

Outlet covers, fabric cords— minutia MATTERS.

It doesn't need to be precious, but it can be considered. Even the hardware store has brown plastic outlet covers that are more attractive than the white ones. I think about these things—about hinges or about getting fabric cords when rewiring a lamp. It's not always authentic to the house, but these things feel like authentic materials.

It's OK to love old things and use new appliances.

You can get great ranges these days, including ones that reference vintage style, but it's an appliance, so buy it for the function, not the look. If you cook, definitely shop with performance in mind.

VINTAGE plumbing fixtures still work today—and with very little effort.

Most people don't know, but sinks, tubs, and toilets were standardized in the 1920s, and measurements for the fittings haven't changed, meaning you can go to any hardware store and get a drain or faucet that fits a tub made in 1929.

There's no reason in the world to buy a NEW sink.

There are so many beautiful old sinks out there in the world if you're OK with a classic or vintage aesthetic. They're not mechanical, they're just vessels, so they can be easily plumbed and brought back to life.

It's EASY to change an unfitted kitchen.

In my kitchen, only the sink would stay in its place—and that's because of the waste line. Everything else in this kitchen could just be removed or rearranged in a single day.

Be uncompromising about the RIGHT thing.

There are and were parts of my home that are unfinished or missing parts for a long time because a cheap compromise feels wrong. It's OK to hold out for the right solution; the answer will turn up at the salvage yard or on eBay if you're keeping an eye out.

Section Four

CHAPTER 22

The Almost-Nothing-New Renovation

Freshening up dated cabinets with a coat of paint, sure. Reupholstering dilapidated chairs, absolutely. But deciding to keep the straight-from-the-'80s red-and-white tiled counters—and even intentionally designing *around* them, well, few of us would be brave enough to try it. Designer Meta Coleman is here to tell you: It'd be a lot cooler if you did.

Eying a less-than-perfect space for the elements you can keep versus what to scrap—that's a thoughtful and responsible approach to renovating, but woefully uncommon. The thing is, salvaging the OK isn't just the environmentally responsible way to go, but actually creatively potent. Limitations, as most artists know, force ingenious solutions.

A shimmering, design-establishment renegade, Meta Coleman turns out decor flexes that inspire awe. She's the type to DIY her own cast metal handles when showrooms and the internet can't turn up what she needs.

The scrappy, ingenious nature of her work has serious roots. She hails from a family of German environmentalists, a mother who didn't throw away food and found utility in just about anything. Meta's approach to interiors feels based on appreciation. It's less about control (she doesn't believe in it) and more about intuition and imperfection. The gift she can offer us is encouraging us to see things for what they are and accepting them as is—or after a coat of paint.

In a Utah midcentury ranch house, Meta kept those tile counters, nearly all the homeowner's furniture (chests, wing chairs, and an aging dining set, too), and made a few moves with paint, including those ceiling beams, and wallpaper (a Josef Frank paper when the quote for hand-printed British stuff came in too high). There were only a handful of purchases, including rattan stools to add texture to the space; the rest was there by the time the designer arrived. This is another case for leaving well enough alone.

Advice on

Ethical remodeling

Unconventional reuse

The power of paint

opposite

Who could be glum in a room with this red? The fiery paint color in this Utah midcentury ranch house was inspired by Swedish painter Carl Larsson, whose domestic scenes are hygge-full and charming. Both the homeowner and the designer enjoy the artist's work. The wallpaper is Josef Frank.

following pages

The former kitchen and dining space was a bit dark and out of step with the vibe of the cool, creative owner, a style-minded artisan and grandmother of many—casual family gatherings number to forty.

The counter tiles, which were existing, are red and white, but the cabinets were painted a non-matching warm yellow white, Benjamin Moore Mayonnaise. The slightly mismatched hues make the room feel more relaxed.

Section Four

209

opposite

The beams were painted at the very end of the project— it wasn't part of the original plan but felt right—and looks it, too! The window coverings have a sweet, simple fabric tape detail.

left

The wing chairs belonged to the owner but were down at the heels. Instead of shopping new, Meta had them rehabbed. A gingham woven fabric (always more durable than a print) is on the interior; a more special fabric by Josef Frank covers the exterior.

below

A proper yellow (here, Farrow & Ball Babouche) is as good as a serious dose of serotonin.

"**LIMITATIONS**, as most artists know, force ingenious solutions."

left

Lovely paper and paint colors! The cabinetry is Geranium, the wainscotting is Boca Raton Blue, and the chair, like the ceiling beams and other details, is Dill Weed, all Benjamin Moore.

below

The tile counters and backsplash, cabinets, and hardware were all existing. The tiles provided a jumping-off point for other design elements.

opposite

A pine hutch just off the kitchen holds the home's blankets and a collection of china the designer picked up to brighten the upper shelves.

following page

The table and chairs were also existing and repaired and painted in Babouche, a beloved Farrow & Ball yellow. The move was inspired by Claude Monet's dining room at Giverny.

214

"META'S APPROACH IS LESS about control (she doesn't believe in it) and more about intuition and imperfection."

Meta Coleman

designer

A kitchen has to be a workhorse but also a SHOW PONY.

That was a request from a client, and it gets at the truth—kitchens are fun to create and also really hard to design. You have to create so much function but also make it feel special.

Mixing creams and whites feels LOOSE.

Don't let the room get too controlled, too matchy. Things need to complement each other, but not be perfect. Slightly mismatching creams and whites in paint feels a little bit more relaxed.

It's a home, not a SHOWROOM.

A bookcase with three books, an object, and then a vase: that's just not realistic. Who collects three books? Of course it's about curating, collecting, and adding layers, but you should also be true to how you live.

Shop appliances IN PERSON.

You can't do this online, you have to go out there and touch and feel and look in order to get a sense of how you'll like living with it. You should ask yourself: How do I cook, who does the cooking, and how do I entertain? Exposure helps you to get a firm idea of what you like.

There are a lot of ways to DO things.

But being overly controlled isn't a good one. It doesn't amount to anything really beautiful. But when you allow the process to happen, and you lean into the imperfections and the challenges, the outcome is better than if you try to control everything. The hardest challenges sometimes turn out with the best outcomes.

Not all inspiration is created EQUAL.

Look for books from or about the time that your home was built, or books by artists who inspire you. Dive deeper than social media.

A SECRET design element is the orientation of the space and the available light.

This house was dark; most of the windows are obstructed by trees, so it gets "green light"; it needed more warmth from the colors inside, so now there's a yellowy white paint.

Kitchen design STRATEGY:

First think about what you want to achieve in that space or what kinds of things you want to happen in that room. And then it's on to problem-solving: listing the problems and figuring out how to make them go away.

When shopping for lighting, think FUNCTION:

Over a dining table you want a cozy mood, so it needs to be low, but you also want it softly diffused, because you don't want a bulb shining in your face. You've got to think about that. Go a bit lower for a pendant over the island, too.

Loosen your GRIP.

You know the feeling when you walk into a room and you feel like you can't touch anything and you can't sit comfortably? You don't want that. You want to feel relaxed and comfortable, and letting go of perfect elements helps that.

Section Four

217

CHAPTER 23

A Case for Not Overdoing It

Keeping the
character

Seeing past
the mess

Not buying
into trend

He has photographed the homes of Louis Armstrong and Anaïs Nin, shoots for A-list publications, and regularly sees modern grandeur up close: book-matched marble backsplashes stretching up a double-height ceiling, walls of refrigeration units, Costco closets scaled as large as . . . Costco. When it comes to selling kitchen success to a larger audience, Chris Mottalini knows how.

But at home in Upstate New York, the photographer keeps it small and low-key in a house made by hand in the 1950s by a master stonemason from the Bronx. "Rough and handmade, cozy and inviting," is how the photographer describes the space. With nothing particularly straight or even, the cabinetry and floor install (which he executed himself) was challenging, but imperfection is not just acceptable but encouraged. Slick and too-fancy design elements were eschewed in favor of humble—albeit custom-made—plywood cabinetry and unvarnished interiors. The rigorous lack of fuss is a bit of a stylistic move, too. Admittedly he says, "I am willing to sacrifice functionality for things to look better." In this kitchen, he didn't have to.

"**TOO-FANCY DESIGN ELEMENTS** were eschewed in favor of humble—albeit custom-made—plywood cabinetry."

In the New York home of photographer Chris Mottalini, the pendant is Sea Gull, now sold through Generation Lighting. That style globe pendant was standard issue in many midcentury houses and is still classic and affordable.

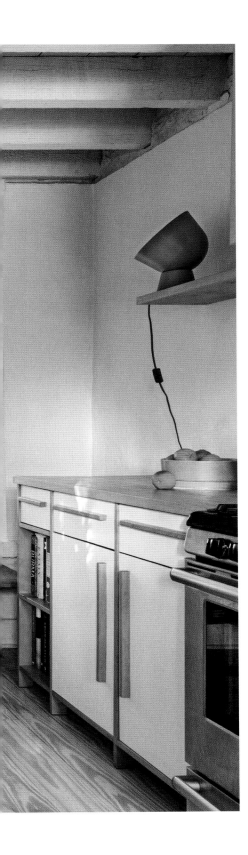

left

The kitchen is small but wide open. With a kid and dog around, Chris disliked the idea of an island or table in the mix. The cabinets and the bench are both by EB Carpentry, a friend's business.

above

The countertops are solid maple, and the cabinets are good-grade plywood with laminate fronts.

Section Four

221

Uncommon Kitchens

Chris Mottalini

photographer

You don't NEED a backsplash.

It's true! Here, it didn't feel right to tile over the texture of the plaster walls. And we didn't need to—every now and then you wash the walls; it's not a big deal.

Choose materials right for your SEASONS.

Marble is everywhere these days, but it's not right for the style of this house nor the climate here in the Northeast. It gets drafty in the winter, and a marble surface would feel freezing and unpleasant to touch.

Less stuff = more ROOM for beauty.

You don't need all those cabinets. You can probably get rid of the fifteen tools and gadgets you don't use. Without them, you might have room for something more beautiful than a cabinet.

Gas is OVER.

Eventually we'll get rid of the gas stove—for environmental reasons and for the benefit of the respiratory health of my family.

If you bought it for character, KEEP IT!

A bunch of chairs came with the house. They weren't perfect, but they're cool enough. If you buy a really cool, kind-of-weird house, don't rush out and purchase immaculate brand-new chairs; consider sticking with something that has character if that was the point.

Can your friends HELP?

The carpenter-artisan we happen to know lives in LA. So he built these cabinets there, flat-packed them, and drove them in a station wagon across the country to this rural part of New York State. We could have never afforded the same thing locally.

Use furniture to keep people OUT of the way.

The bench tells people: If you want to be in the kitchen, hang out over here. It's also multipurpose —since it's at the door, it's the natural place for sitting and putting on shoes and getting ready for the day.

Kids, dog, and island is TOO many.

There's enough happening in the room already; it didn't make sense to have an island interrupt the flow of the space here.

opposite

The ceiling was left exposed; the home builder had laced the wiring through drilled holes—good enough! The walls are plaster; it felt weird to cover them with tile or other backsplash materials, so they're occasionally wiped down to keep clean.

Section Four

223

CHAPTER 24

The Art of Bric-a-Brac

Skip diving has a more elegant ring to it than dumpster diving, but what it's called and even what you find isn't the point—it's how you employ your spoils that matters. And in that, Helma Bongenaar is an A-list skip-diver, outfitting her central Amsterdam home with dazzling finds. Hers is a different way of looking at renovating. Instead of spending the time and energy on plans or shopping or earning money to finance a custom solution, this approach requires relentless creativity, intrepid solution-finding, and tireless flexibility. This is something many creative types can get behind, but even the rest of us have something to learn from this space.

A stylist, chef, and cookbook author, Bongenaar hosts dinner events, but she more frequently hosts her grown children and their partners, the same kids who were once horrified by their parents' penchant for foraging in abandoned lots. Plenty of people who visit congratulate the family for keeping the 1880 spot historically intact. (The home was indeed once a longshoreman's pub.) But everything here is new. Or new-old, that is. The space, the high ceiling, and the big windows demanded a certain approach, says Helma, but the rest is happy experimentation.

Look around—and don't miss the collections. When Helma was a student, she resolved to eat with silver cutlery and from beautiful plates. Purchasing a complete set was out of the question, so it began with second-hand bits and pieces. It grew, and the palette rallied around blue and white. She kept at it. Different profiles, same colors—and now look.

Humble and abundant is the ethos here.

Advice on

Ingenious sourcing

Making feel-good spaces

Building a collection

"**MY HORROR** is a cold, bare kitchen without a pan in sight," says Helma. "Do people live here? Do people cook here?"

opposite

A peek into the Amsterdam home of cookbook author and host Helma Bongenaar. The collection of coffee bowls began when she was a young au pair in Paris. They number more than one hundred; they're all blue and white and fifty to one hundred years old.

Section Four

225

above

Helma and her partner found the mix-and-match cabinets at construction sites and in a dumpster. She developed the paint colors herself.

opposite

Helma keeps her tools displayed. The counter-top is waxed cherry. The backsplash is pieces of marble, found or gifted. The patch of tiles is from a stack of antique ones that hail from Belgium. It was a barter between Helma and a friend; the friend received a carpet.

Helma Bongenaar

cooKbook author
and host

You have to look and listen CAREFULLY— everyone requires a different approach.

The kitchen is where people live, cook, eat, and tell stories. That is always the starting point. Otherwise, there are no rules,

See something you LOVE? Say something.

Walk by renovation sites and ask for what you like! The doors and cabinets here have been "saved" from destruction—and were also completely free!

Displaying COLLECTIONS makes it look as if you've been in your home for ages.

And that feels welcoming. The kitchen is the room where you spend the most time; it has to feel like a warm and safe atmosphere.

Something worth spending on—A COOKER.

A good range is essential—make it functional and beautiful.

Death by PLASTIC!

Use as little plastic as possible. Why not keep everything in old-fashioned glass jars like grocery stores used to? Glass is a perfect material for food storage—you can see what's in your jar but it doesn't take on any smells. And it looks beautiful, too!

Neat cupboard interiors are OVERRATED.

Instead, what about keeping your collection to a color scheme and letting it all stack up?

The very best kitchens are their very OWN;

there are no other kitchens like them. Originality is the best thing to experience in someone's kitchen. The second best thing good kitchens have is a long table to invite friends and family as often as possible.

Decoration, yes, rugs, no. NEVER!

You can stumble over it with a hot pan in your hands. Plus, wood and tile wipe up easily, but dirt is invisible in a rug—and kitchens get dirty!

Remember: A kitchen is a LIVING space.

That's why it's important to make it into something beautiful and lively. The trend toward dark gray is so gloomy and boring.

Southern Europeans have the BEST kitchens

because they're for a culture that prizes real cooking, fresh ingredients, and putting in a lot of time. The rooms are sometimes large and not designed according to the latest trends but instead in ways that let people live and host and really cook.

Section Four

A Midcentury Canvas for a Haul of Antiques

For some, this midcentury "rambler" would be enough of a throwback element, but not so for this family, the mom of which is a vintage lover. She knew the adjacent rooms would have antique rugs and so-called brown furniture, and sought a fresh and crisp Scandi-leaning foundation as to not make the house too period or ye olde feeling.

MK Quinlan believes anything built-in should support the house architecture. "It felt right that everything added in a permanent way would be in sync with its era," says the shop owner and designer, citing the cabinet style and even the stainless steel backsplash. "The workaday nature of it is utilitarian; it just makes sense for the house."

Slab-front cabinets, stacked appliances, and a kitchen table versus an island are hallmarks of kitchens of this era; less so the fresh blue hue (Farrow & Ball Blue Ground), which took two tries to get right. (The first color came off as a powder blue befitting a nursery, and the construction crew and owner walked in and knew right away to scrap it.) But the pop of color was always a definite; "I wanted the house spirited, because that's how we are as a family," says MK. The cheerful color is also a great foil to the old pecan table, Chinese Nichols rug, and antique rack festooned with copper pots and "gathering baskets" for the two preschool kids' foraged stones and greenery—ingredients for fairy salads and dinosaur soup.

left

The Birmingham, Alabama, 1959 ranch-style house of vintage dealer and decorator MK Quinlan. She shares the home with her husband, two little kids, and a dog.

opposite and following pages

The top is a combination microwave-convection oven, the bottom a conventional oven. The "stacked" approach was common in midcentury kitchens. At right is an appliance garage that holds a stand mixer, blender, coffee bean grinder, and more.

left

MK, who has a namesake shop in Birmingham, outfitted her rancher with a midcentury-leaning kitchen and lots of antique furniture.

Slab-front cabinets, Scandinavian in style, says MK, are painted in Farrow & Ball Blue Ground. They are natural wood, not MDF (this is rare!) and were made by Birmingham Woodworks.

above

A peek into the dining room with the pantry to the right and panel-front GE fridge to the left. The antique pecan table was purchased by MK's mom at an estate sale in Birmingham years ago— it's the most loved piece in the house, she says.

Section Four

In the pantry, kids' snacks are kept low for them to retrieve on their own. As it turns out, the strategy wasn't foolproof.

opposite

The family lives at the old dining table; it has marker and paint spots, but it's OK. The bentwood dining chairs were bought without seats; they now have pink seats, a combination of fabric left over from the daughter's room, and a layer of vinyl on top for easy cleaning, a trick she learned from designer Barrie Benson.

MK Quinlan
designer *and* shop owner

Spaghetti sauce vs. art; ART WINS.

For a minute there was a concern about hanging the Peti Clements folk art pieces near the range. What if sauce splashes on them? You have to think the same way about your decoration as you do about clothing—if you're not wearing it and enjoying it, what's the point?

Ample counter space . . . is OVERHYPED.

There's a fear out there that without an island there won't be enough counter space. You don't need it as much as you think you do.

Contrast is KEY.

There are the contemporary-feeling cabinets and the antique elements of the room. That "push and pull" is what makes the room feel dynamic and ageless.

The appliance garage is for your HEALTH.

Moving a stand mixer back and forth is an invitation to ice your back. An appliance garage lets you slide out hulking appliances without bending and lifting.

No to range, yes to GRIDDLE.

One of those enormously expensive old-Europe-style statement ranges didn't make sense for this house. We cook every night—family meals—and the five burners and a griddle for weekend pancakes is more than ample.

Dish DRAWERS—do it.

It's preferable to pull up a heavy stack of plates or bowls from lower versus balancing them from a cabinet up high. There's a reason dish drawers became popular.

Separate the STOVETOP from the oven.

It opens up a whole world. There's a wide, shallow drawer of giant utensils right under the burners, and all the dishes in deep drawers under that. The pot lids are here, too, right near where they need to be!

Fast, cheap solutions can be BETTER than pricey ones.

The pink dining chair fabric was left over from my daughter's Roman shades; a layer of vinyl on top made it suitable for kitchen spills—and the retro look is cute. Sometimes the big-budget things don't turn out the way you want them to, so when you can, save time and money by just using what's on hand.

HELP kids be autonomous in the kitchen.

There are drawers intentionally for their use: one for snacks and art supplies. And the chairs are intentionally lightweight—if they need to get something high, they can pull one over. You can't do that with a heavy counter stool.

A kitchen table is COZY.

It's the most loved and used piece of furniture in the whole house. It's for reading the paper and taking a break and doing homework and art projects and eating, of course. And when friends come over for dinner, it's at that table—it's where everything is and it feels more "us" than hosting in the dining room.

Section Four

239

The Makeshift Kitchen

WHO WOULDN'T WANT TO HANG *out at the "Jungalow by the Mountain," one of designer Justina Blakeney's mold-breaking, bohemian-beautiful spaces? The artist-designer's rooms teem with life (even if you don't have a green thumb) and feel both resolved and offering space for growth. Posting to her many followers, she doesn't shy away from the process by scuttling the grunt work (construction, imperfection) in favor of the "after" picture.*

During the many-times-over delayed renovation of her current home in the foothills north of LA, she revealed she'd been cooking from a makeshift kitchen. There was nothing posturing about it—it looked as stressful as all get-out.

Justina and her fam made it to the other side (tips ahead), but here's a snapshot of what happened as they waited more than a year for permits.

The question was: move into a demolition site with faulty plumbing and no kitchen and begin our new life near the mountains, or stay in our small house and commute an hour to my daughter's new school come fall? We chose the former.

An untimely demolition meant moving in with the plug-in refrigerator that came with the house, but no sink, no dishwasher, no counters. In the beginning, we thought, this isn't that bad! It's like camping.

We set up card tables and pulled out the toaster, rice cooker, hot plate, microwave, and Crock-Pot. We made make simple stews and steamed veggies and rice. And we solved problems as they arrived.

Without a pantry, my husband, who is neat, created boxes and bins for food storage. One bin had things that needed only hot water, like instant noodles or soup; there was another for Ida's school snacks, and so on. But then we started to get ants.

It's not *cooking* that's the most challenging in a makeshift kitchen, it's the cleaning. We were doing dishes in the *bathroom*, and the plumbing was bad, so scraping the plates really well was essential.

We finally bought a slop sink at IKEA and installed it to the hose line outside on the patio so we could really do dishes. The sink drained into our flower beds, so we bought eco-friendly soap to keep those

> "WE QUICKLY learned . . . that's when the bears come."

Uncommon Kitchens

alive. We quickly learned that if there is *any* food at all in the sink over-night, that's when the bears come. That's the thing in the mountains: You can't really put your garbage out. Bears and raccoons break into trash cans, and then there are the possums and skunks.

We try to be sustainable where we can, so we didn't want to use paper plates and plastic for months and months, but, eventually, we were ordering takeout once a day.

The cognitive effects of missing the kitchen were arguably harder than the inconveniences. There used to be this energy around having dinner together. Jason and I would be back from work, Ida would be

During construction: The kitchen was still a folding table, even as the rest of the house was ready for decorating.

back from school, and we'd cook together and talk about our day and connect. But that disintegrated during the renovation and the pandemic, and it got a bit more casual. It made our dining habits less about family and community and more about just *I'm hungry*, and *What shall we make for Ida?*

For us, the difference between a family meal and takeout is that as a family, we share a pot and a bowl, we serve each other and ourselves. With takeout, we'd often have different meals alone—the veggie burger is for this person, the pasta is for . . . You're all serving *yourselves* versus sharing something from the middle of the table. It's fine for some nights, but that vibe weighed on us eventually.

There were things we still enjoyed—we're a big artichoke family, and we still steamed them and enjoyed them together, but prepping other veggies was hard. We're all just really excited to get back into our veggies.

Justina's kitchen inevitably ended up internet famous. Here's what's in her newest:

A VENT HOOD, finally, and now we can cook anything.

A mix of CLOSED AND OPEN SHELVING. Things like food packaging don't need to be displayed.

A BROOM CLOSET. Without one, it's a hassle to find a place for it. This one even has a plug!

A SPOT FOR SMALL APPLIANCES. We finally thought through: Where will the blender go, where does it get plugged in?

ROWS OF PLANTS near the ceiling, a skylight, and piped drip irrigation! Even I got tired of taking down and watering the plants!

A BEVERAGE BAR with purified water and instant hot water; I drink tea all day long.

A dedicated COFFEE BAR for our morning ritual.

An INDUCTION RANGE from Café. No gas, no hot surface—our cat likes to walk across counters!

—Justina Blakeney

*previous page
and above*

The new kitchen, with
Café appliances and
zellige-style tiles for the
backsplash and window
surround.

right

A beverage station for
a family serious about
beverages.

Justina Blakeney
designer, author,
and founder *of* Jungalow

To make it yours fast: VINTAGE.

My homes quickly feel lived-in because there's so much vintage. An older rug on the floor, a vintage tablecloth, and plants, of course. That makes the space feel homey and cozy. Vintage and handmade things feel warm and inviting, not stark and new.

When it feels TOO new:

Try items in a mix of materials and textures. They lend that feeling of character and juxtapose nicely with brand-new things, like marble countertops and the perfect cabinets and new glistening tiles. My mix is wooden salad bowls, super-thick purple ceramic plates, and my collection of green Moroccan tamegroute pottery, which is wonky and imperfect.

Not everything of integrity needs to be STORED AWAY.

Having quality pieces on display lends to the feeling of handmade and authenticity.

How to create a PERSONAL kitchen:

What are your rituals? And your family rituals? Drinking tea all day long is one of mine, so we did the instant-hot-water tap. Jason is big on making soups and stews, so there's a pot filler. We both are big coffee drinkers, so we have a dedicated space for that morning ritual. And we love to host, so we're expecting the house to often be full of people, and we want them to feel comfortable enough to help themselves, so there's a beverage station.

Looking to the FUTURE . . .

we went with an induction range. We want our home to be solar-powered eventually, and so we weren't going to do gas, even though that's what we've always had.

If you call yourself a COLLECTOR:

It's OK to go overboard with the amount of stuff you have. I'm the type of person that wants fifteen kinds of trays and beautiful salad bowls. My impulse is: What a pretty bowl . . . I want it! I'm a collector and admirer of beautiful things, and most of it's affordable or vintage. But my partner will ask, Why do we have twenty-five salad bowls, and which can I get rid of? I'm a collector, he's a minimalist.

To compromise, my "OVERFLOW"

collection of bowls gets styled on the hutch in my home office, and I bust them out for Thanksgiving or other big holiday moments. Win/win.

To have MORE control over your space:

Go for multifunctional things, or fewer. Our wall oven also has microwave functions, so there is one fewer appliance on the counter. I'd rather have plants in those spaces.

Section Four

A short parable about an author undertaking a kitchen renovation while writing a book about kitchens:

The kitchen was what drew me to our last house. It was big and sunny and in that aesthetic netherworld between the early '60s and the early '90s, with white slab-front wood cabinet doors, those great $3 wood handles from the hardware store, melamine counters, that type of glass globe pendant light that was standard issue at the time, and turquoise-painted drywall. The owner, Gael, who raised four girls there, later told me that she'd shown her painter a tile as a reference and returned home from vacation to find the room "more Caribbean" than she expected.

As it turned out, the room couldn't be kept as is or even rejiggered. There was aging, questionable electrical snaking behind the cupboards and laced through the beams. To repair it meant taking it all down—and the cabinets weren't strong enough to make the journey back up again. We'd have to start from scratch, which left an opportunity to remove the ceiling tiles, lay a floor, and find a new owner for the 1950s Cook-o-matic that worked just fine.

> "I was living in the room equivalent of a mullet."

Design cues in other parts of the 1905 house made paint and decorating choices easy. There was oak trim throughout, a pair of hexagonal rooms, and a parlor with crown moldings so dramatic they were practically designed as a dare to other neighborhood living rooms. They were classical rooms, and I knew the rules and how to break them beautifully. But the kitchen would be brought down to the studs and required a new vision.

I began with appliance research (my most discerning design-professional friends led me to Fisher & Paykel—done) and the first thing to catch my eye was the brand's plucky crimson-colored range, nicely analog-feeling with round dials,

We nixed the backsplash in favor of continuing the run of lime plaster walls. The induction stove is Fisher & Paykel, chosen because it's healthy and safe near kids (and chefs love it).

The after picture of my own breakfast nook—well, at least where I left off. The plaster finish is lime plaster, artfully painted on by Venosa Interiors. Together we chose how much variation and movement the brushstrokes would show. The chairs are Zone, a Quebec retailer. The blue stool with doves was painted by my mum in a near-periwinkle blue that's popular in our house. The Lucia pendant from Visual Comfort hangs overhead and a vintage secretary is at back. Stylist Darina Bellini set the table with linens from Maison de Vacances.

but with induction technology, a priority to me. In the end I chose its glossy black counterpart, but the idea of barn red stayed. Concurrently my designer Celia Bryson was feeling the red idea and suggested oxblood cabinetry. Of the two colors we tested, Dinner Party Red and Hodley Red, both Benjamin Moore, Hodley came out on top. Soapstone counters from a remnant slab (cheaper!) and a work table in a contrast color (Farrow & Ball Down Pipe) kept it from feeling like a color-coordinated bedroom set, but damn if this half of the kitchen wasn't the nicest thing I've ever owned. With zero funds left to do much of anything other than buy a thank-you-I'm-sorry-but-we-must-stop-immediately for Celia, I was living in the room equivalent of a mullet. The cabinetry and appliances were fabulous and done (Celia's domain), and then a freshly dry-walled box bereft of personality or charm—the breakfast room. As it turned out, that half of the

"My kitchen is a teen with a promising future—not fully formed, not fully at peace with itself."

kitchen was not just going to decorate itself with its high ceilings and sunny disposition; it was in desperate need of the warmth and gravitas elsewhere in the house.

Were you surprised I hired a decorator? Know this: I've written about design for twenty years to the day, meaning, I know exactly that I am not one. A decorator would have anticipated the missteps I was about to make.

There are crown moldings throughout the house and in the cabinetry, but none in the breakfast room. I OK'd more modern slab window moldings on the deep-inset windows. These are not here nor there. I could have done none—it can feel very historic—or echo the molding profiles in the other rooms in the house.

The ceilings are high. TOO HIGH. Answer: a pendant. But I wasn't informed enough to request that the wiring for the pendant be a separate line from the overhead can lights. This meant the pendant couldn't be illuminated on its own, which is much more lovely. (Answer: I unscrewed the overheads.)

Acres of drywall. Oh, it's deadly. (If you're ever feeling, like, why is my house sort of meh, ask yourself how much drywall there

248

is and do anything you can to correct that: art, temporary wallpaper, a plaster treatment . . .)

But here's what I was smart enough to enact on my own:

Window coverings. Venetians in self-lined, semiopaque performance linen; simple and soft. (OK, this was Celia's idea.)

Art. Just tack. it. up! Something to look at on those big walls. Mirrors, too—mirrors help!

A racetrack table. This one is old IKEA. Dining tables that are too wide are lousy for conversation. Narrow models (circa 35" wide vs. the usual 45") are extra good for conversation.

Furniture. A secretary that didn't have a home but that works well for bill-paying and card-writing. To be honest: It's for storage, I just keep the stuff there and do my paperwork at the table.

Runners and rugs. I'm Team Rug. I shake it out, spot-clean it, it's not gross.

Lamps. The working title for this book was practically *Just Put a Lamp in Your Kitchen*.

And a few others that took me a while to arrive at but that nonetheless started to bring it together:

Wall treatment: A lime plaster by a specialist added the age that the room lacked, and the luminous-at-lunch, sexy-at-supper vibe of a fleshy pink. Meow!

Paint the limp, bland window molding the same color as the wall (based on Benjamin Moore Monticello Rose) to make it disappear into the wall. It's an active way of ignoring bad architecture.

Paint the ceiling one step down paler pink. You say you can't tell, but when you're in there, you can. The cans/exterior of the lights are also painted! The switch plates? Painted.

And here's where I left off—a wish list:

A vintage bench or settee to break up the chairs

An indoor-outdoor rug to mitigate noise (the downside of high ceilings)

A fresh hue on the beautiful crown of the Visual Comfort light— why not?

My kitchen is a teen with a promising future. It's not fully formed, not fully at peace with itself. My design hijinks were almost all of the same nature: trying to become as natural and comfortable as where it started. Pushing it to be itself, to gel into a single feeling instead of a bunch of design choices and budget lines. The lime wash was entirely to add warmth, patina, and age into the space. A shortcut to turning the hands on the clock! The rest of it just takes time.

This kitchen offers two lessons: (1) Sometimes there's no place like home. Gael had kitchen #1 right, and it took a long time and money to get back to half as good. (2) There are easy ways to counter a white box: paint, art, rugs, curtains, stuff! You can bring a bit of vibe to an empty space with not too much money or fuss.

The point is: Go easy on yourself, find small ways to improve on the existing, and lean into the process. If you can make cereal or tea, find a spot to lean or sit, and something pretty to rest your eyes on, your kitchen is doing exactly what it should be doing.

TOO LONG; DIDN'T READ

A short list of easy, happy additions to any kitchen:

A houseplant potted in a vintage vessel

A small piece of art in an expected spot

A warmer, brighter bulb over the sink or island

A jar of wooden spoons

A few brightly colored dish towels

A small throw rug in front of the sink

A single chair in a lonely corner

A stack of cookbooks

Some tunes or a little NPR

Prettier vessels for the food in the fridge

Hang an heirloom plate

A small collection of vases or jars on a sill or ledge

Taper candles of all different colors (Light them at breakfast!)

A pretty pitcher and water cup (healthy!)

Put the OJ or iced tea in a clear or decorative container instead

Lay a bright dishcloth beneath veggies in your produce drawer

Let your island or table wear a tablecloth, just for the day

A friend or neighbor at the table

A closer look at the Reath Design kitchen featured on the back cover.

CONTRIBUTORS

Nancy Cavaliere, the ultimate homegirl, was instrumental in bringing this to life.

And the designers, home-owners, and photographers behind these stories:

Commune Design

Libby Cameron

Frances Merrill

Nicolò Castellini Baldissera

Jaqui Seerman

Marta Chrapka

Poppy Lissiman

Tomas Daviet

Dorian Caffot de Fawes

Victoria Sass

Katie Rosenfeld

Shavonda Gardner

Jessica Rhodes

Casey Kenyon

Christine Flynn

Agnes Rudzite

Nate McBride

Heidi Caillier

Scot Meacham Wood

Hendricks Churchill

Libby Cameron

Geremia Design

Robin Henry

Eppie Thompson

Laurel Consuelo Broughton

Liz MacPhail

George Saumarez Smith

Rob Ashford

Kevin Ryan

Rodman Primack

RP Miller

James Coviello

Meta Coleman

Chris Mottalini

Helma Bongenaar

MK Quinlan

Justina Blakeney

James Gardner

ACKNOWLEDGMENTS

This book is for Teddy & Whitaker, and to Greg, for those two gifts and countless others, including the time and support for my writing this.

Thank you to my editor, Shawna Mullen, whose valuable reader insights, scathing wit, and inexhaustible patience proved the irresistible combination needed to inspire a book from me.

And thanks to the many folks whose passion for design and living has shaped my work: Lulu Powers and Stevie Danelian, Newell Turner, Richard Ekstract, Jonathan Adler, James Laforce, and Stephen Henderson . . .

To my mum, Bettyna, and sis Louisa, forever painting the kitchen and everything else.

To the folks at the Westmount Public Library, the Bibliothèque et Archives Nationales du Québec, Hotel Mont Gabriel, and the Matawinie—glorious Québec, turning out spindrifts for me to gaze at while I write. Look!

PHOTOGRAPHY CREDITS

Stephen Kent Johnson: cover, 12, 190–196

Patrick Biller: 1, 8, 11, 112–118, 246–249

Laure Joliet: 7, 14, 18–24, 159, 160–166, 253, back cover

Nicolò Castellini Baldissera: 16–30

Chris Mottalini: 17, 78–79, 108–110, 126, 183–188, 218–222

Jess Isaac: 32–38

Colombe Studio and PION Studio: 40–48

Trevor Tondro: 51

Jack Lovel: 52–58

Michael Paul: 61–62

Wing Ho: 64–72

Park & Oak: 74

Read McKendree/JBSA: 81–90, 130–138

Shavonda Gardner: 92–96

Elizabeth Haynes: 98–106

Agnes Rudzite Interiors: 120–122

Lindsay Brown: 124, 168–174

Lesley Unruh: 128

Nick Johnson: 141–150

Eppie Thompson: 152–156

George Saumarez Smith: 177–178

Julia D'Agostino: 180

James Coviello: 198–206

Chanté Vaughn: 208–216

Helma Bongenaar: 224–228

Laurey Glenn: 230–238

Justina Blakeney: 241–244

Editor: Shawna Mullen
Designer: Deb Wood
Design Manager: Danny Maloney
Managing Editor: Glenn Ramirez
Production Manager: Kathleen Gaffney

Library of Congress Control
Number: 2022940693

ISBN: 978-1-4197-6231-4
eISBN: 978-1-64700-712-6

Text copyright © 2023
    Sophie Donelson
For photography credits,
    see page 255

Cover © 2023 Abrams

Printed and bound in China
10 9 8 7 6 5 4 3 2 1

Abrams books are available at
special discounts when purchased
in quantity for premiums and
promotions as well as fundraising
or educational use. Special
editions can also be created
to specification. For details,
contact specialsales@abramsbooks.
com or the address below.

Abrams® is a registered trademark
of Harry N. Abrams, Inc.

ABRAMS The Art of Books
195 Broadway, New York, NY 10007
abramsbooks.com